MOUNTAIN

MOUNTAIN

Exploring Britain's High Places

Griff Rhys Jones

MICHAEL JOSEPH
an imprint of
PENGUIN BOOKS

Published by the Penguin Group

Penguin Books Ltd, 80 Strand, London WC2R 0RL, England

Penguin Group (USA) Inc., 375 Hudson Street, New York, New York 10014, USA

Penguin Group (Canada), 90 Eglinton Avenue East, Suite 700, Toronto, Ontario, Canada M4P 2Y3 (a division of Pearson Penguin Canada Inc.)

Penguin Ireland, 25 St Stephen's Green, Dublin 2, Ireland (a division of Penguin Books Ltd)

Penguin Group (Australia), 250 Camberwell Road, Camberwell, Victoria 3124, Australia (a division of Pearson Australia Group Pty Ltd)

Penguin Books India Pvt Ltd, 11 Community Centre, Panchsheel Park, New Delhi – 110 017, India

Penguin Group (NZ), 67 Apollo Drive, Rosedale, North Shore 0632, New Zealand (a division of Pearson New Zealand Ltd)

Penguin Books (South Africa) (Pty) Ltd, 24 Sturdee Avenue, Rosebank, Johannesburg 2196, South Africa

Penguin Books Ltd, Registered Offices: 80 Strand, London WC2R 0RL, England

www.penguin.com

Published in 2007

Copyright © Griff Rhys Jones, 2007

The moral right of the author has been asserted

Produced for Michael Joseph by Essential Works
www.essentialworks.co.uk

Printed in Great Britain by Butler & Tanner

A CIP catalogue record for this book is available from the British Library

ISBN: 978-0-718-14989-5

CONTENTS

INTRODUCTION

I was actually at a meeting to talk about something else entirely when somebody suggested that I could present a programme about mountains for the BBC. 'But I know nothing about mountains,' I bleated.

'That's excellent,' the executive replied. 'It will be a new experience for you.'

'But isn't there a certain amount of skill involved?'

'Well, we can see you mastering those.'

'And if I don't master them?'

'That's good television.'

So I was recruited, or press-ganged even. This is the story of that trip, which took up a lot of 2006, but it is obviously not a mountaineer's account. I was a virgin climber and a trembling one. I had once crawled up the volcano Stromboli hoping to dodge fridge-sized rocks. I had been skiing in various parts of Switzerland. I had even crossed the High Atlas in a Fiat Punto. I thought I knew what a mountain was like. I was wrong. Now I have climbed fifteen British mountains, some of them three or four times in a row for the cameras. I have scrambled, bouldered and scaled. By climbers' standards, of course, I have done nothing, but I do feel, well … experienced.

As a virgin, I was a little sceptical to begin with. Was the discomfort going to be worth the effort? Apart from a little panting, could it really make a man of me? Was I really going to walk down my flat city streets with a new glint in my eye and a swagger in my step? You can judge for yourself. There were some minor physical challenges, to which I usually failed to rise, and a smattering of minor orgasmic summiteering moments. But what began to fascinate me as an outsider was the history of the vertical world I encountered. By walking into the hills I discovered that mountains are a separate environment, a different territory with their own

rules, where for thousands of years people have lived, but with difficulty, where bad men have fled, where dreamers have escaped, where ordinary people have struggled to survive and where elements of everyday existence long since abandoned on the easy flat lands have hung on right up to the present age. And on every climb there came a moment when we crossed a stile or climbed a wet gully or breasted a ridge when we suddenly broke through into an undisturbed, wild place, bare, open, ravaged by previous ice ages and largely left to itself: a real wilderness on an over-crowded island.

Almost a third of our country is covered in mountains. This is a minor introduction to some of the people who have been there and lived there. It would have astonished Mr Tarrant in the fifth form but I did become fascinated by the way that geography can affect our lives and shape our history. British hills hatched rebellions, attracted speculators, sheltered eccentrics, powered industry and prompted scientific investigation. So there is a little bit of that sort of stuff here, in among the subjective whimpers and triumphs.

Of course I didn't go on my own. Cubby, Mark, Fraser and other experts were with me all the time. They not only showed me the ropes, lovely purple ones too, but listened to my wild prattling and suffered my prickly inexperience. There were cameramen and assistant producers and directors too who struggled up slopes and sheltered in wet hotels. They are largely hidden in this account, as they were in the resulting series. But one thing rather frightened me, a portent of the new media reality, I suppose. In all our bold company I was definitely the oldest person in the unit. 'Are you all right, Griff?' was too common an enquiry. 'Yes, thank you. I'm only fifty-four,' was a grumpy common response. It took my wife to point out to me that I was in fact only fifty-two. I couldn't really hide my inadequacy behind pretend advanced old age. Damn.

But at the end of months of trudging and exploring, climbing and clambering, I have to admit that this fifty-two-year-old virgin was left with one inescapable question. 'What took me so long?' The hills were an extraordinary and unexpected experience and as I sit here writing this I find I am hankering to go back. I hope, when you read this account, you will be able to see why.

NORTH-WEST
SCOTLAND

CHAPTER ONE

North-West Scotland

Crouched in a Cessna at ten thousand feet I could finally understand why blokes with preposterous facial hair called aircraft 'crates'. The doors were aluminium straws with a shell of silver paper. If I leaned too hard against the side I was going to leave my own shape pressed in the frame. The entire plane seemed to bend and crumple as we flipped around like a paper bag in a wind tunnel.

My pilot's company was running out of Loch Lomond. 'We're going to take tourists, fishermen and landowners out to the furthest isles,' he shouted over the roar. Now he was taking me by the quickest route to the far north west of Britain.

As we crawled around massive lumps of hill and thundered laboriously along valleys neutralized with snow, I dimly realized that that thin cotton thread of a line across the bottom was the main road between Altnaharra and Inverness. On the map there was satisfying emptiness, and emptiness in our crowded island is rare, except that – and I apologize if this seems blunderingly obvious – it wasn't empty. The space was filled by mountains – an upthrusting territory that needed endurance to cross. True, the airplane could curve effortlessly around that beetling cliff. A car, with its powerful built-in laziness, could slip straight up hills and down the other side. But the road followed the line of least resistance and added miles to a journey, snaking round the low route, avoiding heavy, difficult climbs. These ranges I was flying through were in truth just as inhospitable as those mid-European Alps I had crossed so many times by giant jet-liner.

Six hundred miles from London, on this white day, approaching the slinky, silver Kyle of Tongue, we were descending on the very tip of Sutherland, a place

ABOVE: The far north west of Scotland has more in common with the Arctic than with Esher.

more akin to the wastes of Greenland than the rest of Europe. Beyond the mule-grey skin of the estuary itself, the freezing North Atlantic stretched away to the next hard surface – the polar cap. We breasted the western edge, turned and slewed downwards on to the water in a cascade of freezing white. At the head of the huge shallow lagoon a broken nose rose up against a darkening sky. This was Ben Loyal. Any reservations I may have felt about the status of British mountainhood were blown away in a slithering vista unfolding through a veil of spray.

I stepped gingerly on to a float and into a boat. Andy Beveridge was waiting to take me to the shore. He was a razor-clam fisherman. The kyle was a silted harbour. There was a causeway bisecting it and the road ran across and off along south to Lairg. Ben Loyal dominated his working beat.

There are, of course, greater ranges in Europe. The Matterhorn is higher by two miles. But as anybody who has gone skiing knows, the route to the high slopes in the Alps happens via miles of foothills and lesser bumps. Here 2000 feet of crumpled horn rose straight from sea level. It was magnificent. Andy saw me looking.

'Are you going up it?'

'No,' I shrugged. I was going to try to get up Ben Hope, out of sight and round the corner. Ben Loyal may have been imperious but at 2865 feet it wasn't high enough even to count as a Munro, the name given to any mountain in Scotland over 3000 feet, in honour of the man who first set out to map and climb them all, Hugh Munro. There are 284 Munros. The trick now is to do them in one single month, or backwards, or without a break. Ben Hope was to be my first. But Ben Loyal, the lesser peak, was enough to cow me into silence. 'What about you?' I asked after a while.

'Oh aye, I've done it with the kids, you know, as a holiday thing. It's a good view, if you get it.'

He meant that the mists came down and obscured the peak so frequently that we were lucky to see the mountain clearly now.

'You can see it better sometimes in the winter. But it'll be cold up there, I should think.'

This from a man who, if he hadn't been picking me up, would have been, even on this raw day, down over the side, with an air supply in his gob, sifting through the sand to drag up the long, boxy shellfish for the Chinese restaurant trade.

LEFT: A stone landing, a freezing cold loch and the magnificence of Ben Loyal behind. Not a day for razor clams.

That night in my tiny room in Tongue I laid out my own kit and re-read my *Basic Guide to Hill Walking*. Nine hundred pages of close print – not bad for an activity I had mastered reasonably effectively since I was two. This was another testament to the otherness of the mountains. Ninety-nine per cent of the book was warning. Warning about the weather, warning about the cold, warning about the accident potential of loose stone, or hard stone (slippery), or steep grass (even more slippery). The ease with which people can get lost. The difficulty of finding a way in fog. The foolishness of blowing a whistle for pleasure (when the tooting whistle may be the only hope of rescue). Planning, pre-planning, eating, sleeping; everything was intrinsically unsafe or deadly. The entire book seemed designed to frighten people off.

For the first time I tried to sort out what I had brought with me, under instruction, as it were. My collection of kit covered the bed, the floor and parts of the wall. I certainly didn't want to take everything up a mountain, if at all possible. The anorak was obviously useful, except that it was no longer an anorak. It was a 'shell'. The science of dressing, presumably after close consultation with the Mothers' Union, had been subject to injunctions about being nice and warm, and 'feeling the benefit'.

First there was a base layer. I had some of that. The secret is not to sweat and yet to be warm, to enclose but still to breathe. Having swathed oneself in light but breathable fabric, tight against the skin, this was covered with that woolly stand-by: the fleece, in various thicknesses, one for climbing and one for standing about in, which meant the alternative was bunged into the knapsack. (Sorry, I call my backpack a 'knapsack' from some nagging folk memory. What is a 'knap' anyway?) There were heavy, unyielding boots with laces that went right down to the toes. There were some peculiar flappy things made of Gore-tex, called gaiters, which zipped and strapped around the boots in a simple fashion, if you allowed for about six hours of fiddling. My trousers were, even then, merely a shell, because I had some super-tight, Laurence-Olivier-as-Richard-III, black leggings to wrap over my bulging calves, and a pair of excellent nubbly socks to go on top.

I had everything I needed. My immediate problem was that I had everything I didn't need as well. Obviously I was going to be cold. So I had packed all those multi-coloured thermal long underpants and woolly socks that we had

accumulated skiing. They were not very scientifically packed. A number of them actually belonged to my wife – probably the ones with the lacy trim.

But the clothing was as nothing. There were drinking bags with catheter-like tubes for sipping at the vital supplies of water (dehydration was a great enemy on the mountainside), head-lights for descending, gloves, spare pairs of gloves, whistles, flasks for spare water, map cases, food in silvery plastic bags, compasses, emergency rations, blankets, lip salve, junk, more junk and a single ski pole, supposedly important for balance and control. This was a serious business.

ABOVE: My first ascent in nubbly socks.

It snowed in the night. I woke a little light-headed. The breakfast weather forecast announced that the coldest place in the whole of Britain had been at minus eighteen. That was us. We were that minus sign.

By the immutable law of accommodation, half the film crew were staying in another hotel. Somehow we had to get together. I dressed in every layer, as instructed, and waddled out into the magic kingdom of crunchy whiteness, looking and feeling a little like Buzz Aldrin. Scott, my driver, ex-special forces and a former intelligence agent, heaved me into the front of the hired Vauxhall. The wheels spun excitedly. The snow rose around us.

At that moment a snowplough came thundering along. They had cleared the roads as far as Altnaharra. It was standard practice: the mail and the papers had to get through. Scott asked whether the plough could clear the back route round to the side of Ben Hope.

Alex the driver puckered his face under his bobble hat. 'Not usually, no. What are you wanting out that way?' The farmer had his own four-wheel-drive. He usually cleared the route with a tractor.

'We're going up Ben Hope.'

'Not in this weather you're not.'

'I think we'll be able to manage it.'

'No, you don't understand me. You're not going up! I work for the Mountain Rescue.'

Scott began to explain that we were all right. This was television. We had a talisman. We would be escorted by the rest of the Mountain Rescue team.

The snowplough man seemed unconvinced. The Astra was stuck anyway. But luckily the hotel owner had a four-wheel-drive, gas-guzzling behemoth. This was no status vehicle. It was essential in Sutherland. It certainly was to anyone who wanted to climb Ben Hope in a blizzard.

It was nine miles to the bottom of the mountain, through a landscape of monotone textures. Between Altnaharra and Tongue, the snow added a smoothing effect, but the lochs and burns were wrinkled ammonite at one end and sharp, frozen blue at the other.

A small wooden sign announced 'Ben Hope' and pointed the way across a trackless snow field. It seemed incongruous. We were now, I guessed, standing in what would usually be a demarcated car park for the casual rambler. A broad river valley wound away to the north. There was a distant huddle of farm buildings, but the valley was otherwise empty and blanked by the snow. It looked prehistoric, except that, perched on an outcrop of high land commanding a view both ways, was a round stone fortress built originally by the Picts. So it was actually historic.

This valley had been worth defending for some 3000 years. Around the time the fort was built it would have been largely cleared of trees. The bleak, primeval emptiness was an illusion. It was empty by human choice. Indeed it would have been snowy like this, in a permanent manner, only 12,000 years ago, at the end of the last ice age. It is now believed that the huge frozen ice field that covered this place, and the sea beyond as far as the pole, the force that gouged out the valley where we stood, may well have melted in the space of a few decades around 10,000 BC. It was probably followed by a period of extremely palatable global warming, certainly warm enough to bring early hunters and nomads up here pretty quickly.

I was going up 3040 feet with Cameron McNeish, a writer, adventurer and Munro-bagger with a nice beard and an infectious enthusiasm, who laughed at my onion skins of clothing and persuaded me to take off one of my fleeces. 'It is sensible to set off feeling slightly cold,' he explained. 'You'll get hot soon enough and find yourself sweating.'

Cameron has been editor of *The Great Outdoors* magazine since 1991. He completed his first round of Munros in the same year. This was a walk in the park for him.

He took my ski pole, showed me how to twist out the telescopic extensions to the right length and we trudged off, beginning by following, as was so often to become the case, a watercourse cutting down the mountain and providing a handy cascade of rocks to climb.

We had bargained for bad weather and now we had it. One hundred and forty-four schools across Scotland were shut that morning. By the evening the A roads would be closed. Luckily it wasn't blowing any frosty winds as we left. There was blue sky overhead, deformed by towering, grey-black cumulus, and littered with a spattering of flakes. The stream fell down through black pools heavy with ice and dotted with spectacular miniature waterfalls of icicles.

'It's arctic mountaineering up here,' Cameron said proudly, 'because the winds come straight from the Pole. These…' and he pointed up at the beetling broken pointed summit, 'are arctic mountains.' I stuck out my lower lip and nodded.

There were probably no more than a dozen trees on the entirety of Ben Hope and they were crouched down in the cleft where we started, frosted and sugared with snow. Cameron picked his way ahead through the rocks and ice and I followed dutifully, reminded of Good King Wenceslas as I trod in his deep foot holes.

I was like a child, though, unwilling to settle in for the long haul. Impatient and frisky, I had glimpsed the peak through a break in the clouds. It looked impressively high and alpine, but somehow I could hardly conceive the sort of journey this was going to be. I was jigging on, thrusting ahead a little, probably keen to impress Cameron with my own enthusiasm, but this was going to be a proper trek and there would be distance and effort involved.

'You always gain height surprisingly quickly,' Cameron remarked. And he was right. We had been puffing on for no more than fifteen minutes but the perspective was already changing. Other peaks were emerging above the horizon. The valley now seemed way below us. The Pictish fort had shrunk to a thimble in the white landscape. Already I was feeling exuberant. We were heading up and away from people and roads. There were no hedges to cross or gates to shut. We were up in an abandoned waste. To the west, the ledge we were on lifted up and followed the top of a huge black cliff. The wind picked up. As we clambered higher, tiny icy balls of compacted snow, hard and stinging, flew in our faces. 'Graupple,' said Cameron.

Typically this was a Swiss-German term, like 'rucksack' or 'alpenstock'. The sport of climbing had been developed and refined by the British when we were the rich and adventurous centre of the civilized world. But the tough and foolhardy young men who pioneered the sport in the 1850s had done so in the Alps. Hugh Munro had climbed these British mountains in the late nineteenth century. The Scottish Mountaineering Club was not even founded until 1889.

'God's chandeliers,' said Cameron, pointing at the bulbous configurations of icicles in the frozen waterfalls, but also God's transparent undersea creatures, or God's Polish art glassware. It was steep going. I was no longer feeling snug or smug. I was grunting for breath a bit and beginning to sweat.

'Sweat kills,' Cameron joked.

I nodded ruefully. I had started nice and warm, now I was red-faced and perspiring and fearful to stop in case I suddenly became a popsicle.

'But there's no real danger at these temperatures,' Cameron said.

RIGHT: A pristine roof with a blizzard in the offing.

Above the first stepped rock face we came to a cliff and ran at it, yomping upwards through deep snow, clutching at heather buried just beneath the surface to get a handhold, but walking as if on air, upwards to gain a ridge which would take us on and away to the left. It was utterly unsullied. This was soft, crisp, snowball snow underfoot, good carving and building snow – 'quite unusual', Cameron told me – supportive and totally blanketing and obliterating all the paths that might have been there before. Here in winter with the ice fields stretching out to the horizon it felt as if we were the first who ever walked on this surface, instead of a couple of ramblers on a well-worn path.

But who had actually been the first to climb this mountain? All the Scottish peaks are carefully recorded. Most are claimed or attributed to individuals, by no means all of them climbers. Bonnie Prince Charlie was an original Munro-bagger, heading north away from his failed coup, with the Redcoats on his trail, escaping

into the hills and in the process, according to the record collectors, conquering summits across the Highlands. Botanists and geologists and map makers, especially map makers, followed. General William Roy made a map for military purposes in 1765 and this was used for the first recorded ascent of Ben Hope, by James Robertson, looking for botanical specimens in 1767.

Already we had left even the certainties of paths and heather behind. Now we were up where the rocks had fallen from the heights and formed unearthly piles and alien environments. The granite was naturally cut into planes and squares.

The slopes themselves weren't difficult. Each field stretched ahead like a pristine roof. We slogged on and surmounted the ridge and I stood for a moment with Cameron, savouring the inescapable truth that this was not, as I had thought, the last.

'There's another peak, then.'

'Aye. Two or three more, I can't remember.'

False summit followed false summit. The day which had begun so fresh and new had become dark and used and grimy. Snow was blowing up, down and around us and we had lost all vision beyond a few feet ahead. So much so that I failed to notice that we had reached the top. There was a slope, a field of stones and ahead of us a cairn. All sense of the massive and awe-inspiring had been lost in this grey cloud of fog and snow. Only the ground beneath our feet gave us any sense of up or down. If there were a view of seven counties or 300 other Munros, or Greenland, or my house, it was utterly obscured. We might as well have been at ground level, except for the details. There was a squared-off block with inset brass furrows at the very highest level, a trig point, and growing out of its top at a horizontal angle were little white coral sticks, with pine-cone spandrels, sharp and organic, just a few centimetres long but exquisitely fashioned.

'That's rime,' Cameron explained.

The wind and the ice formed these fairy ice-lollies. So this was rime.

Cameron was already backing off through the swirling fog. 'Come on.'

'What! We came all this way!'

'It's getting dark.'

Was it? I found it quite difficult to tell. We were in danger of becoming 'benighted' – a word which, I now realized, meant being overtaken by the night

and was a state to be avoided by any traveller, even one in nubbly socks. So we groped around in our packs, got out our miner's-lamp head torches and headed back down the mountain almost as soon as we had got up. If we had brought some skis we could have been down in ten minutes. As it was, we plunged through the drifts and let ourselves slide on our boots and bottoms as best we could for a further couple of hours.

That night, slumped in front of a fire in the hotel, I had to accept that all this felt like an achievement, though there was none to boast about. When the first 'sport' climbers went up into the Alps for the sake of the experience instead of gathering useful scientific information, *The Times* railed in a leader against the 'selfishness and recklessness' of their enterprise. They had exposed themselves to

ABOVE: 'Hither, page, and stand by me.' I follow trustingly in Cameron's footsteps.

ABOVE: Ben Hope later in the spring with the pictish fort Dun Dornaigil Broch in the foreground.

needless danger and frightened their families, and to no good purpose (no *Basic Guide to Hill Walking*).

The next morning I went to the local Skerray post office to meet Meg Telfer and Marilyn McFadyen, both incomers. It was a pretty place with a thatched roof, held on by stones on strings, and painstakingly restored with a grant from the National Lottery. I knew this before Marilyn told me because there was a thumping great sign disfiguring one entire gable end.

'We have to have it. It's a condition,' she explained.

But the girls were otherwise happy in their new role as joint postmistresses to eighty-three people, and as I write this I hope they survive the threatened cull. They were more than an indulgence for the people in this remote area. Shops which sold more than tartan tourist rugs and biscuit boxes were few in number. Meg had come to Sutherland precisely because she wanted to climb in the mountains. She had all the kit and loads of maps. Marilyn, by contrast, didn't worry about them at all. She had no particular urge to clamber up rocks.

'Meg tells me what I'm missing, but I know what I'm missing,' she said.

'What are you missing?' I asked.

'Sweat, exhaustion, terror, exposure, chill,' she replied. That was what tourists like me suffered.

I was only at the post office because I was waiting for postman Paul Blackman. He drove up, delivered his sack of mail and opened the rear door of his van for me to get in. This was the 'post bus'. There wasn't much room in the back, just a couple of comfortable seats. It was a means of transportation so civilized and intelligent, generally on time and combining several vital needs, that I can only assume it will be done away with fairly shortly.

Paul was an incomer too. He came from Swindon. But he found dating someone from Altnaharra a bit of a schlep. So he moved here, and married into a crofting family. He had some sheep of his own now, so he was extremely patient with the stock that tended to wander haplessly out in front of us in the seaboard areas. He had time to be a shepherd because his rounds didn't start until ten. I didn't ask, but assumed that he couldn't start until ten because his post didn't arrive until then.

The service was introduced in 1968. There are 140 routes which between them travel two million miles and carry 80,000 passengers annually.

Paul loved the scenery, how the colours and the ambience were always changing. As we talked, they did. The weather surged over the low hills. The road wound through lumpy mounds of blackened heather which had absorbed more of the snow, so they had a piebald marking. But all along the coast the mood changed in a flash, the colours pulsed like sea anemones with the passing complications of the clouds. A distant view of the mountains was translucent blue, ice blue, the same blue that glows like a gas pilot flame at the bottom of holes in the snow high on the slopes. The water of a burn was a pale slab of turquoise. There was a sudden patch of yellow reeds or exposed grass. The sky was piling up with fast-moving clouds, burning gold at their edges and reflecting in the drifts of snow blowing up on the ridges.

'And if you go up to Caithness it suddenly becomes flat and completely different,' Paul said.

Mind you, it wasn't the flat I was there for. Paul was another one who never went up the mountains himself. He dropped tourists who did, with their backpacks, sometimes carrying bags of coal to take to outlying bothies. But he never wanted to join them. I could see why.

This was supreme happiness for me, trundling along with the daily round, with Paul chatting away in the front, and playing down his role as Santa in a red van. It occurred to me that he was the major connection with the modern world of consumer durables for a whole section of the population. We were in catalogue country and Paul was the courier.

'I expect you're pretty busy at Christmas, Paul.'

Paul cackled.

We travelled some fifteen miles. It was only a tiny part of Paul's daily round trip of almost ninety miles (from Thurso to Tongue and back), taking me past Loch Eriboll, the sea loch where the British Navy had stationed frigates and submarines during the Second World War, and now a single fishing boat huddled by the remains of the old fortifications. On the far side I got out and walked the rest of the way to Lotte Glob's house, perched on the side of the inlet.

Squat, bulbous, amorphous figures sat within a rolling enclosure and beyond the gate lay a scattering of huts, the centrepiece of which was a very fine building

RIGHT: Looking south from the Black Cuillins on Skye.

indeed, with a curved roof and slatted wooden sides. It was deliberately constructed to evoke the simplicity of a farm outbuilding, pure and direct – raised on stilts and enhancing the grand sweep of the loch. This was Lotte's workshop and atelier.

I envied the house. It had a Scandinavian modern practicality. Not unexpected because Lotte was a Dane, although the award-winning place was in fact designed by a Scot – Gokay Deveci. I had probably even seen it before, in the pages of a glossy magazine. Beyond the entrance were two small rooms and a kitchen. Beyond that a narrow corridor suddenly broke out into a wonderful double-height space, a sleeping platform at one end, and a glass wall that opened on to a balcony at the other; and the overwhelming vista of the loch itself, still streaked with snow, beyond.

Lotte had achieved her dream home on a tiny budget, paid for by her work as an artist. She was a potter. Her speciality was ceramics. But her fascination was the hills around her. She snorted at my book on hill walking. 'I call them Munro commuters,' she said. 'Sometimes I pass them and they are always in such a hurry, puffing on, you know.' She imitated a walker pumping his arms.

She would have sent a shudder through the authors of my guide. She liked to set off, armed with little more than her sleeping bag and a week's supply of food, in order to wander at will. 'I don't think these people understand the mystery of this place at all. I go to get deliberately lost.'

Lotte and I crunched across the snowy garden to her workshops. One kiln was wood-fired. It was boxed in by heaps of kindling. The other, inside a shed, looked like a large, blue, metal electric safe. It could reach temperatures of 1320° Centigrade. Lotte showed me some of her 'books', leaves of clay cut with her writings and interspersed with flat stones, which had been fused together in the white heat, and then a piece of granite that had been through the furnace: a heavy blob of molten rock, the edges dripping like candle wax, shiny and slippery. Of course rock could melt. It had melted originally. I knew that. Up until that moment, though, looking at the splodginess of the molten granite which had squeezed out of the layers of Lotte's firings like cream from a sponge, I had never really considered the cookery involved. The mountains I was exploring were wrinkles in a hot crust on a lava lamp suspended in space. It was this relationship between naked geology and human creation that Lotte was exploring in her pieces.

One by-product of her experiments had been to produce globes of clay, hollow inside and rock-like outside. They could float. We walked out by the side of a lochan to take part in one of her 'interventions', clambering over a sheep fence and

efficiency. She saw the lands over which she had virtually feudal control as a means of paying for her upkeep, if only the inconvenient people who lived there could be got out of the way, and an up-to-date, modern, agricultural monoculture introduced – sheep, in fact. Sheep everywhere, mowing the uplands, eating any young trees and taking the bark off the rest, creating the bare, neatly shorn landscape we recognize as Scotland today. The sheep population rose from 300,000 to 1,600,000 in fifty years. Only a third of the human population remains, even today.

The Countess was not alone. The Highland Clearances were a nationwide drive for new productivity. But the Duchess of Sutherland had the zeal of a nineteenth-century Iron Lady. She achieved her ends by harrying people out of their cottages on to 'marginal lands', basically the edges of the estates, the unproductive bits, where those who didn't escape to America were encouraged to struggle for a living by fishing or crofting.

Walking through the stunted remains of the deserted village, a sharp wind drifting snow into the remains of the houses, I could understand how the Clearances still fostered resentment. Allan MacRae was a direct descendant of the families thrown out by the wicked Countess. He still farmed the land by the high road. He has 125 acres of rough ground and some of the prettiest calves in Scotland. We fed them, tipping pellets into troughs and dodging their coy dinner queue barges, while he told me how he had led a successful campaign to secure the grazing rights to the hills beyond his own fenced land. A local land association, the Assynt Foundation, bought 21,000 acres, using their own money as well as government grants. The land was actually the crofters' own common grazing, which just happened to be owned by someone else. It is sparse upland. The sheep and cattle have to wander on the range. Allan works this land, and now the land association is his landlord. He hasn't even really bought the freehold. His croft still remains what someone defined as 'a small parcel of land surrounded by regulations'.

Allan made me a cup of tea in the house he had built himself and leaned across from his chair to fix me with a glittering eye.

'You know that road from Ullapool to Lochinver. What is it? It's thirty miles from one village to another. It should be farmed. There should be houses all along there and people living in those houses and making that land productive.'

The urban conservationist in me bridled a bit. I leaned in myself. 'What, you mean new buildings, new houses, all along that lovely road?'

'Aye. There were people who lived there once. They should be encouraged to come back.' He delivered his killer punch. 'Listen. It's not your wilderness! It's my wilderness. It's not here for people to drive through and admire. It should be used. It's good, productive land, not like this…' He gestured at his own acres, which were part rock, part cliff and wholly a tipped-up table. 'My family were driven out on to this poor land, no more than subsistence.'

Allan sat on crofting committees. He was on the Highland Council. He battled for the Highlander with a fierce, committed pride and lived a cold, active, difficult life which he obviously relished. 'It is a hard life. They say we have to "diversify". That's the word they use. We have to find other jobs. But there aren't any other jobs.'

I felt guilty that I was staying that night with an incomer landlord, and doubly guilty, because Count Adam Knuth was such a charming, civilized host, living in a delightful house, who cared deeply about his land.

His housekeeper, Helen, welcomed me at the door of Loch Loyal Lodge. I had passed it several times, solitary and solid, a faintly suburban Victorian building,

like a pointy rectory, just off the road in a small stand of mature trees.

Count Knuth had bought his house fifteen years before. It came with an oversized garden, which happened to include a mountain, the whole of Ben Loyal. We met in the porch. The count was tall. He spoke impeccable English (not rare for a Dane) and dressed more like an English gentleman than most English gentlemen, in blue cords and a stripy shirt. The house was more of a log-cabin lodge inside than the outside might have promised, being panelled throughout in pitch pine; lovely stuff too, with a dark, plain, orange glow.

The count had bought his spread when the Duke of Sutherland had been forced by death duties to sell off some of his land. A map, which covered most of the wall in the hallway, showed the parcel that he got. It ran the entire stretch of the road I had travelled. Who wouldn't have bought it, given the resources and the chance? When his aunt died and some of the forests that she owned became available to him, the count decided to sell them off and acquire a considerable chunk of wild country here in Scotland instead. 'I swapped a pension fund for a mountain. What could I do with a load of paper pulp?'

Wilderness was rare, and he wanted to hunt. The results of this hobby were all around us. There were a dozen horned heads on the opposite wall. We went through to the small dining room, with a fire in the grate, and a selection of stuffed birds and small mammals watched us, with glass eyes, as we munched estate-reared venison. They certainly didn't all come from the slopes of Ben Loyal, unless various exotic antelopes had been let loose up there.

The maintenance of his herd and his hobby cost the count a lot of money. For the time being, the wilderness was not my wilderness or Allan MacRae's wilderness but Count Knuth's wilderness, though Scottish parliamentarians may do something to disabuse him of that in the future. He seemed to have few objections to ramblers walking over the country and became quite misty-eyed over its beauty and appeal.

He also offered me a bed for the night. I climbed a polished staircase to a pretty room with yellow wallpaper, where a huge and magnificently antlered okapi mournfully eyeballed me from above the wardrobe.

It was not good weather for stalking the next morning, nor for wearing my stalking outfit, a head-to-toe overall of mysteriously random zigzag leaf patterns. It

LEFT: Allan MacRae and the author arrive for lunch.

gave me a headache to look at my own trousers. The hills were still covered with snow and I would be visible from 1000 yards, but Ian Smart, the chief stalker, was taking me out to get a flavour of the effort involved.

It was a formality, but he expected me to shoot at a target before we went. This was what everybody had to do. If a visitor could get three bullets in a circle, they could be let loose on the hill. Count Knuth himself was an excellent shot. So I was handed a rifle with the usual instructions about bolts and safety catches, and flopped down in the snow.

Reader, I hit my target. I expect you're as startled as the director, but, long before drink and progressive music took their toll, I had spent a wasted youth training in the school CCF. Pull firmly into the shoulder, get the little sight at the end of the barrel in the middle of the 'v' at the back (or in this case the cross-hairs on the telescopic sight straight on the wobbly bit of paper), breathe out, relax and squeeze the trigger.

Hawk-eyed as I was, I would have been permitted to help cull the herd, but I was handed a camera instead. And off we went, hunting photographs.

When there is snow in the Highlands, the deer come down to the roadside at night to lick salt. Their golden eyes may be the last thing you see in the headlights before a twelve-point monarch of the glen joins you in the front seat of your car. We had passed plenty of them after dark, out on the roads of Sutherland. They're limber and they usually bound straight over the deer-proof fences, but some, so they say, try to jump the headlights instead. It gives road-kill new meaning.

That morning, as a result of the snow, they were still hanging around the lower areas. A successful stag will field a massive harem, plus their young. As the young males (the bucks) grow, so they become aggressive and want a harem of their own. Then they start fighting. Humans intervene and sort out the dispute by shooting a few of them for the pot. But it is not easy.

They look out for intruders, especially ones in lurid-green leafy suits walking across the snow. Deer are extremely shy. We could see them all right, but it was an effort to get close enough to effectively shoot them with my camera.

Ian led the way, trotting across the snow, with me scuttling behind, plunging into drifts and tripping over hidden tussocks and trying to control the volume of my creaking bones. Just as suddenly he threw himself to the ground and we crawled forward on our bellies, digging our own snowplough furrows for twenty yards or so. We breasted the hillock and peered ahead, between a few strands of yellow grass. Alas, the deer were not as stupid as they looked. They had run down the hill, along a gully, and were now about a quarter of a mile behind us, looking nervously in our general direction.

I was already freezing. I had compacted snow all down the front of my camouflage jacket and my fingers had become like frozen carrots. Thank goodness I had only to squeeze my button and not steady a rifle. But Ian was off again. He had done this before. He could propel himself along the ground like a vole. I slithered after him, scooping buckets of slush up into my sleeves on the way. We got into a frozen bog and waited. Hours passed. After a little while the herd descended into the valley ahead of us. This was my moment. I raised my site. I extended my telephoto lens to its full extent. I squeezed the trigger and popped off a few out-of-focus and wobbly shots of a startled-looking deer.

The deer were certainly part of the ancient history of this place. They 'belonged' there. Unlike the sabre-toothed tiger, the beaver, the wolf and the brown bear, however, they continued in residence because of their sporting potential.

I was to meet people who snorted at the hunters and the landowners and their expensive maintenance of the landscape. To them, they were the successors of the aristocrats who preferred sheep to people. The debate about ownership, control and use of the uplands is run on some very basic issues. Some talk airily of 'Nature' and 'the Wild' (I certainly do), but now I was driving south through an empty expanse of black cliff, windswept top and soggy valley which defied the notion of 'natural'. Was it more natural to have herds of deer roaming the mountains than wolves? In the natural world the deer were kept in check by natural predators. In the natural world the valleys would have been clothed with forest. Perhaps this was a wholly artificial wild place, after all.

Suilven is a more isolated and wild mountain than most. It is called 'the helmet mountain' – a 2895-feet-high shark's fin of granite that juts straight up out of a waste of 'lochan and bochan' near Ullapool. It is not the highest mountain in the region, but it has an unmistakable brooding outline and was used by the Vikings as a navigation point. We were still short of daylight and we needed to make an early start, so we trekked out in the late afternoon to settle into a bothy for the night. I felt a little like Doctor Johnson on his Highland tour, keen to play down the magnificence of the scenery on either side as only a weary southerner can, trudging onwards, grumbling away at the inconvenience of carrying my own coal.

The bothy, maintained by the Mountain Shelter Association, had formerly been a shepherd's hut, six miles from the nearest village, but was in itself a symbol of depopulation, because it wasn't a wicked countess who turned the shepherd out of this little house – it was a wicked Land Rover. The development of all-terrain vehicles during the Second World War enabled farmers to get to their sheep from further afield. Today it is a snowcat, a moon buggy with eight fat wheels, that can most easily cross the mud and the slush, and lumber up a one-in-five incline with hardly a cough. Snowcats were carrying all our filming equipment past us while we soldiered on, singing marching songs.

Eventually we came to the long, low, stone-walled hut with a tin roof. It was black inside. We lit our fire, started up our gas canister lights and I wandered round the dungeon, a frozen Count of Monte Cristo, holding up the lantern and looking at the scratched messages on the bare walls. All I found were names. There was a sort of wooden sleeping shelf to one side and a beaten earth floor, oh, and a book of instructions about digging shit pits well away from the house and clearing up afterwards so as to leave the place properly bare and unwelcoming for the next visitor.

I finally got to eat my boil-in-a-bag meal and it was utterly and surprisingly scrumptious. So much so that I wished I had brought another one. The fire glowed a fierce red but gave out no heat at all unless I was prepared to sit on it. As the temperature plummeted, I stepped outside and found a bright, moonlit night. The frozen hump of the mountain glittered against the stars like a massive silver dome. I could think of few places more satisfactory to be; certainly not inside, where it was appreciably colder, despite the fire. Presumably it would take several days, or a nuclear reactor, before the frozen boulders of the wall would do anything other than refrigerate the inhabitants.

Of course, I wasn't on my own. We were pretending. There was the bloke making the film and his assistant and the sound man and the director, the researcher, several mountain guides and Scott. And they all snored. I intended to set up a midnight creep, on camera, to show the viewer the whole troop rustling and farting like a pack of huskies in the gloom of the shed, but once I was in my sleeping bag nothing would get me out again. My head stuck out like a throbbing snowball, but the rest of me was tolerably warm.

I should have stuck at it. I got up to throw more coal on the fire at about two in

the morning, and I finally dropped off to sleep around five. The next thing I remember was Scott, my ex-special-forces factotum, noisily leaving the hut. I got up too, assuming it was reveille. It was five-thirty. Scott, despite his army background, hadn't been able to sleep at all. He had given up trying.

We had breakfast. I did my teeth in a cup. We waited for my guide to arrive in the snowcat. (He had been put up in the local bed and breakfast.) We read the visitors' book, a catalogue of dope smokers and disappointed walkers. Very few seemed ever to get a view from Suilven. In summer the top was usually shrouded in a dense mist, out of which swarms of vengeful, biting insects descended to eat climbers. As a pale-red sun rose into a clear winter sky and my toes defrosted, I reflected that this cold season seemed much the better option for the bothy and the wild. I began to look forward to the snow hole I had been promised the next week.

'You'll be well comfortable in that,' Scott told me. 'It's much warmer.'

I was to go up Suilven accompanied by a geophysicist Peter Nienow, who now came ambling along the track, charming, lanky and tall. Peter is an expert on glaciation, so I showed him my face and we started walking. He walked for pleasure. His mum had been with him the last time he climbed Suilven. This

ABOVE: The shark's fin of Suilven.

somewhat reassured me, though he told me it had been too foggy to look down, otherwise, he thought, she might have been frightened. This de-assured me.

Suilven looked steeper than Ben Hope. We stepped across a virgin field of crisp snow with Peter in a charming ecstasy most of the way. 'This is such lovely stuff, this snow,' he warbled. 'It's real skiing snow. Not at all the sort of thing you get around here. This is alpine snow.'

We pricked our tracks around a frozen loch and started the last approach to a sheer cliff. Peter pointed ahead to a split in the face of the mountain. It was the gully we were going to use. The cleft would give us access to rock falls and cracks.

I wanted him to explain the geological process that had formed Suilven, and waded straight into a mental snowdrift.

There were so many layers to consider. We were currently walking across Torridonian sandstone – not so much the remains of an eruption in the crust of the earth but a rearrangement of some debris of mountains that had first been thrust to the surface 400 million years ago, somewhere else on the planet entirely, which had then been at the bottom of a long-disappeared sea. The mountains had once been higher than Everest, but that was a brain-unsettling age ago, and a series of accidents and periods of frozen cold had worn away the gaps between them. Phew.

Peter was perfectly equipped to explain and annotate each and every stage of this process. He had a host of elaborate and polysyllabic names at his command. But I found a polar cap forming over my frontal lobes.

The trouble with geology, it seemed to me, and I now set out to explain this to Peter, was that it was an attempt to classify a continuous process. 'Some rock has poured up from molten depths far below, some has been piled up by the plates of the earth crashing together, you see, Peter,' I started. 'But it is not a thing in itself, so much as a stage in a thing, if you see my point. Isn't it hopeless to try to pin down every single stage; like trying to name eddies in a stream?'

Peter smiled and nodded. (He was, after all, on television).

Having outlined my excuse for not learning any difficult names, I explained that what interested me at that moment, apart from Peter's rather splendid hat, was the much more simple connection between these desolate and wild places and the questions that they posed to anyone who walked in them. The monstrous presence of the mountains could not but make people wonder: How did they

come to be? What caused this?

'Mountains were once considered, by the medieval mind, to be "God's mistake",' Peter explained. 'Once God was taken out of the equation then something else had to be responsible. It was no longer sufficient to rely on supernatural causes.'

Mountains themselves had played a part in the development of science. They told us how old the earth was. They made us question how old the sun was, then the universe. Considering he was a professional geologist, Peter was remarkably tolerant of my ill-informed metaphysical discussion. What could be better than a walk like this, for this sort of waffle? And I hadn't even been smoking marijuana in the bothy.

'I can get my head around the fact that the rocks were created three billion years ago, but all that Stephen Hawking stuff is boggling,' said Peter candidly.

ABOVE: Peter Nienow, a geologist, listens to my theories about the creation of the earth.

The gully shut us up. This was not so easy. For most of its height we could make our own steps in the snow, but as we neared the breast of the mountain it became steeper. Peter started wielding his ice axe and I got mine out too, feeling a little silly with this unaccustomed lump of aluminium in my hand. I was expected to hold it the right way too, like a walking stick with too large a handle, the serrated point facing back, trailing it on the inside edge, poking the stick into the drift as we gingerly stalked sideways across the slope. The original 'alpenstock' had been a much longer thing. This anchor-shaped object seemed preposterously dwarfish, but its principle purpose, apart from providing a little extra balance, was to act as an emergency brake.

On the ice, should you slip, you can gather way at surprising speed. Imagine slithering downwards towards the precipice until you become a human avalanche. Fingers won't stop you. A boot is ineffective. It would probably turn you upside down. The long pick-axe end of an ice axe might just arrest things, if dug in hard. So you are supposed to hug it into the chest as you topple and apply all your weight, until the point digs in and brings you to a halt. Got it? Sure?

I tried to conjure the panic that would overwhelm me if I did fall and whizz off down the slope, and the presence of mind I would need to assume the position and hold the axe against my body. All I could foresee was a spasm of flailing limbs and an axe yanked out my grasp.

Then I dropped a biscuit. This insubstantial thing bounced and plunged out of sight in a millisecond. It was steep.

The last bit of the slope was vertiginous. It was like stepping up the roof of a cathedral covered in snow, without even a gutter to rely on. Underfoot I could feel that the snow lay on top of stones which wobbled and clanked softly. I was using not just my axe, but my gloved paws, scrabbling a little at the flat wall of snow at shoulder height as the slope narrowed, and I was feeling frightened. As we clambered up the last bit I was not entirely reassured to find that we had not surmounted a plateau, but a ridge.

Ordinarily, I imagine, Suilven feels little more than a hill with attitude – a jolly Sunday afternoon walk with your mum, or Peter's mum – but I began to find its layer of ice a touch distracting.

We had to climb now – 'a little light clambering' – and the stones were slippery underfoot. They were covered with snow and my new boots felt cumbersome, the pack on my back unbalanced and my ice axe an unhappy burden.

We stepped up across the first heap and then along the side until we came to a sort of bridge to the next col and the proper summit of the mountain. I had to lower myself down and then traverse a thin wedge of earth to get there, except that to do that I had to sit on my arse on the snow and drop myself over a muddy, slippery tussock down on to a small patch of wet, muddy ice at the edge of the precipice, and suddenly I felt horribly, horribly insecure.

The manoeuvre was no more complicated than clambering down from a rather high chair, balanced on a slippery, slightly angled platform. But error had a desperate finality attached to it. There was no margin. The ridge was no more than fifteen feet long. On either side the cliff dropped away totally. The wall of rock fell away without break for nearly 1500 feet.

I tried to persuade myself that there was really no more chance of falling off than there might be in falling off a footpath or tumbling off a pavement into a road. 'But if you did (if you did, if you did…)' the difference was extreme. If I missed, if I stumbled, if I slid slightly, if one boot sluiced out of control, if I just caught my heel, if the snow on that grassy bit was a little icy underfoot. Just one slip, just one novice's mistake, that's all it took.

I let myself slide and got my feet on to the mud. And lurched. And wavered and stopped. I waited while the iron bands around my chest relaxed a little. Then I teetered a couple of steps towards the narrow bridge.

But I had to wait. The cameraman wanted to go ahead. The director held him by the belt and while Simon balanced the camera on his shoulder and looked through nothing but the eyepiece the two of them walked backwards along the ridge, filming me as I dithered on the other side. I felt silly. A cold depression clutched at me. I will be doing this again in a minute or so, going the other way. What's the point of this? What's the point?

The point was the summit. We crossed without incident. On the other side the very top of the pillar mountain was crested with more heaped stone and we clambered up that until we reached a platform the size of a football field. It was so astonishingly flat and smooth that my whole body felt as if it had been tricked. The sky had a winter clarity. We could see range after range of mountains stretching away like a frozen, white, turbulent sea.

What we were really looking at was a series of troughs. 'You can see the direction of the glacial flow,' Peter pointed out.

The other side of the valley was striated like corrugated black cardboard dusted with sugar. The Torridonian rock we were on was 400 million years old in places but the ice cap had covered this area, way above our heads, and had unleashed great, grinding rivers of ice and rock to wear away these Highlands. It had been here only 10,000 years ago, hardly any time at all in the great scheme of things.

That night we sipped mugs of asparagus soup in the kitchen of Glencanisp Lodge, having scrambled down the hill in the dark; lighting the way with our head torches. The big house was owned by the little people these days, who bustled around us. The local land association had bought this wilderness and everything in it. They were going to graze their sheep there and were looking into ways to exploit the tourist interest. The old order was changing.

It was changing on Skye as well. Some 120 miles further south and a little bit west, the island, looked at on the map, was far bigger than I had imagined, and stretched up to wide expanses fifty miles to the north. But at the bottom end, Skye is separated from the mainland by a tiny strait. Looking at the new bridge arching smoothly over that gap, it seemed surprising that they took so long to build it. But half the islanders never wanted it. To them the separation was and is everything.

I wasn't going to take the bridge. I was going the ancient way. I was going to row over in a little boat. I would quite happily have rowed myself. I like rowing, but it was still a long way and a boatman had been found who had rowed the Atlantic when such things were considered utterly, utterly barmy.

Tom McClean lives and works in a little nook of a sea loch, which opens out to a view of Skye. The opposite bank is the edge of the Knoydart peninsula. This is another proper wilderness – some 17,000 acres of forest and mountain – and I had a fierce hankering to explore it, as I watched it slip by a mile to the north.

Another incomer, Tom had been in the SAS. He had seen what Robin Knox-Johnston was up to and did a bit of that solo, mad stuff himself, in smaller and smaller boats. His camp, now disappearing on the shore behind us, had a number of his former vessels lying on the grass, like beached trophies, including a top-heavy-looking fishing boat, reconstructed in the shape of a whale, and a tiny twelve-foot sailing cruiser, a little truncated, given that, in order to go for the record for the smallest vessel to sail across the Atlantic at the time, Tom had simply taken a chainsaw to the stern.

RIGHT: Halfway up Am Basteir, with the island of Skye in the background.

'Well, you know yourself, Griff,' he told me, picking up on my limited sailing experience, 'the waves are not really frightening at all, because once you're out there they're just like mountains, huge hills, which you are climbing up and then going down the other side.'

Applying himself to his oars now, Tom entertained me with stories. How, after his first epic row, he had been washed ashore on the remote Irish coast on a Sunday and had had the greatest difficulty persuading an old lady in a coastguard cottage to open her door and speak to him. And how, on another adventure, he had managed to winch himself on to Rockall for a forty-day visit to claim it for the British Empire, despite breaking his arm in the process. These days he runs Outward Bound courses for inner-city kids. He seemed unconvinced by inner-city initiatives and outreach programmes and believed in long walks and porridge instead. 'No sugar and they soon calm down,' he said.

But, living on the edge of the wilderness, seven miles from his nearest neighbour, he knew that everyone knew about him and he knew about everyone else. 'If you want to be really isolated, then go and live in a big city.'

Tom was just the sort of man you'd need if you wanted to do something mad. He was that British Army uncle figure, always looking out for whoever he was

with, seemingly incapable of panic, though there was nothing terrifying about our adventure now. We crept around the bottom of Skye. This was how, in 1746, Bonnie Prince Charlie had made his celebrated escape 'over the sea to Skye', rowed by Flora MacDonald.

After defeat at Culloden, the Young Pretender spent months crossing the mountains. It wasn't just that his supporters lived there. It was the terrain itself that favoured him. Skye had been his last refuge. When Boswell and Doctor Johnson arrived there twenty-seven years later, they sought out Flora, by then an old woman, to have a look at this legendary heroine of the old way, a way that their very presence in the region showed was passing.

Rowing round the bottom of Skye, I could see the island of Raasay, where Boswell finally climbed a mountain and executed a jig. Doctor Johnson stayed on the ground. Urban intellectuals had yet to celebrate the romance and adventure of rugged scenery. Johnson was still an eighteenth-century, Enlightenment, metropolitan man. He favoured the power of the human mind to control Nature. To him, *Sturm and Drang* were merely wet and noisy.

I rather hope that even the good doctor would have been moved by Loch na Cuilce had he ever rowed into it, as I did, on that flat March morning. This was pure Wagner, or perhaps more accurately, Mendelssohn. I wanted *Götterdämmerung* playing. I wanted repetitive bass notes as we drifted on our oars and slunk inshore.

The water was black and silky. Dolorous, jagged rocks, thick with slimy weed, projected from it and bubbled with eddies just beneath the slow surge of the surface. Flabby seals broke though the heaving basin and watched us like dogs, or rolled back on their platform rocks like lazy nudists. Walls of black granite rose up to disappear in clouds some 2000 feet above our heads. Sometimes the mists parted and revealed a broken peak, so much higher than I had expected, that I broke our self-imposed silence and grunted at the unnerving spectacle. These were the Black Cuillins, the most fearsome, awesome mountains in Britain, not because they are the highest, but because they are, like the Alps, sheer pinnacles of unforgiving rock, rising in crumbling cliffs of granite straight out of the ground in a sinuous eight-mile-long ridge. And they are for sale.

The following morning I read the estate agent's beautiful brochure in a café

LEFT: The Cuillin range is for sale – viewing by appointment.

opposite Dunvegan Castle. It was quite straightforward. The range came with a few small bothies and a farmhouse and covered around thirty-five square miles. It was a world-famous natural phenomenon. I was advised to make an appointment with the Edinburgh office before viewing, though it was clearly visible from almost anywhere on the island. There were several footpaths that crossed directly over the Black Cuillins which, if I bought them, I would have to maintain. The cost? About thirty million.

I was interested and went to call. Overlooking an estuary with high walls and surrounded by a dried moat, despite being prettified and expanded into a rambling country house in the nineteenth century, the castle was still a difficult place to get into. John MacLeod of MacLeod was waiting for me. Wearing a kilt but speaking with the accents of the home counties, he took me on a tour of the castle, through the beautifully appointed private apartments hung with full-length portraits of his ancestors, some of whom, like him, wore tartan.

He showed me the well which enabled the place to withstand sieges. We toured the sitting rooms furnished with chintz, redolent of the comfortable age when his great grandfather had married into an American shipping fortune and brought to the family what they were beginning to lack then – money. It had meant that they were able to live like the lords they were for a few more generations. But as we wound on through this huge place, the gilt became water-damaged. Striding through the upper bedroom corridors, we started to negotiate buckets. The nursery and the children's bedrooms were dripping still and great patches of ruined plaster were dangling from the ceiling.

'It's the roof,' my host explained.

He led me up a spiral staircase and outside through a turret door.

'I have acres of roof to maintain and it was originally laid in copper. It has reached the end of its life. I have to maintain this place. It is a Grade One listed monument. I have to pay for the roof somehow, so it's either lose the castle or lose the mountains. If I could just sell the Cuillins I would be able to pay for all the repairs to the castle.'

It was spitting with rain. We stared across the wet, featureless, rolling hills towards the mountain range. Perhaps some homesick exile in the States would step forward and buy these black-crested smudges, but they have their own mountains

LEFT: Close to, the peaks of the Skye mountains stand up like rotting teeth.

and wildernesses in America to choose from. The sale was widely believed to be a ploy. The laird wanted the John Muir Trust or a Lottery group or the National Trust to buy the mountains for the nation. He was asking just enough to secure his tenure in the castle. But the nation currently found the price a wee bit steep. There had been no takers. Sadly, before the programme was broadcast, John died. He will never see that roof repainted.

The next morning, I visited a school and attended a lesson in Gaelic. Thirteen children were being taught the language in a perfectly ordinary cuboid schoolroom and they, in their turn, tried to teach me just to pronounce the names of each of the major mountains. Am Basteir, 'the executioner'; Sgurr a Ghreadaich, 'the peak of torment'; An Garbh-choire, 'the wild cauldron'; Sgurr Alasdair, 'Alexander's peak'; Sgurr nan Gillean, 'peak of the young men'.

We chanted them together and I got them wrong. Then they chatted away in English to me, but they were perfectly serious about the language, which isn't like Welsh or even Irish. Very, very few people speak it. Almost no one uses it as a first language. One of the boys was the son of the member of a Gaelic band, but not all of the kids were there for obvious romantic purposes. Two of the little girls were the daughters of a flying dentist who did complicated work in outlying islands. They liked speaking Gaelic because they could talk to each other without their mother eavesdropping.

The Gaelic language was something rare and beautiful. It symbolized what their parents and many others across the island were searching to retain – almost especially if they were incomers – and that was the difference. The bridges and the motorways and the tourists and the television were homogenizing the world and losing the independence of Skye.

My hotel had a pepperpot tower at one end, but was otherwise a sort of thirties resort in a moderately sized car park. As I went in, the first thing I encountered, before the extremely pretty receptionist, was a relief model of the Cuillins range, divided into the Black Cuillins and the Red Cuillins. It had been poked about enough to eat away the papier mâché in places. It was the black that interested me, even though on the relief map they had been painted an undercoat grey. The mountains formed a sort of dragon's back, undulating away in a sinuous line, the peaks joined by ridges.

ABOVE: John and I look at a fine Scottish laird dressed as a tin of shortbread.
BELOW: Gaelic as she is spoke.

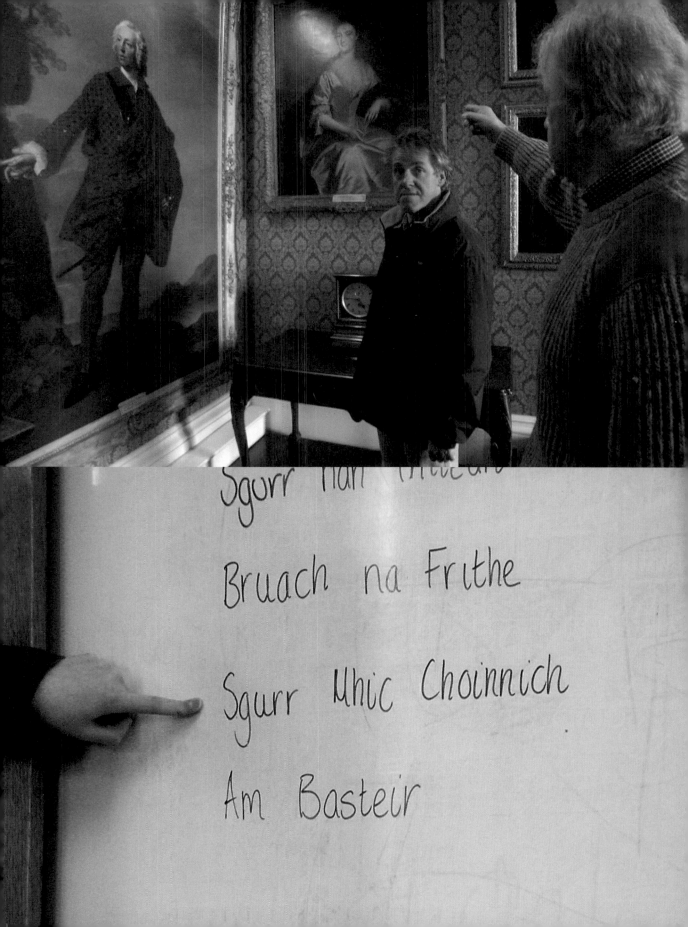

It is highly unlikely that many souls had ventured up on to those craggy outcrops before the climbers came in the late nineteenth century. Hence the Mecca for climbers. Hence the concern of my beloved wife.

'The Inaccessible Pinnacle,' she gasped. She had looked it up on the internet.

'It's rated "severe to very difficult" in winter,' she said and started looking through the list. 'The Buttress, the Devil's Chimney.' They all sounded horrible. 'And you are so feeble.'

In the hotel, just beyond the reception and the pretty receptionist there is an exhibition which tells the story of climbing in the Cuillins. It is a stirring tale, with some significant heroes, who were excited to discover that this part of their native land compared favourably with the Alps. Foremost among them was a man called Norman Collie, who led the way up some of the more formidable peaks, taking a local man, John Mackenzie, as a guide and companion. Collie was a scientist and dour by reputation and Mackenzie was a silent local. They were eventually buried side by side having mapped out most of the Black Cuillins together.

I wondered whether I could, by rights, venture into the bar of the Sligachan Hotel. It was full of climbers and I didn't even have an anecdote. The Mountain Rescue Team met me in the bar. They were gentlemen. Seonachan (Jonathan)

ABOVE: The sun shone continuously on the next-door mountain.

MacLeod, Eoghain (Ewan) McKinnon and Richard McGuire. Priestly figures almost. Like three cultured cardinals. A beautiful way of speaking they had about them too, measured and musical, with a little low, fluting brogue in the tone.

Richard was younger, more the acolyte, the sharp, intelligent one. He drove the mobile library, he explained. It wasn't always easy for him to stop and rush off, leaving in mid-paragraph, as it were. In the high season the rescue team could be called out two or three times a week. But they were mountain-loving men, all of them, and they liked going up.

I think it helped that, for them, their sport was a little frightening. They were amused by my shock at this. Surely I wanted the thrill of being close to death from time to time, didn't I? It wasn't just the challenge. Pushing yourself was not enough. After all, you can push yourself to the limit running – but a failure on the track doesn't kill you.

I think I had assumed that when they reached their level of expertise, it would be the exercising of their skill that fascinated them, but this wasn't really the case. They wanted to get to grips with their own mortality, to hang on to it with one hand, to look down at a 2000-foot drop as their 'fingers began to straighten' while they searched for a hold to take them on. And these were men who went up to find people in trouble.

Seonachan had worked it out. In his time of service, he reckoned the Cuillins had claimed eighty lives. That's two a year. And they smiled slightly weird, rueful smiles at the capriciousness of rocks. They talked of chipped bones and boulders bouncing down erratically, on unpredictable trajectories, from places far up above – dislodged perhaps by sheep as easily as men – and unavoidable.

One poor fellow had been found beneath a mighty stone near Knight's Pinnacle. Hundreds of climbers had successfully negotiated this boulder in the past, but he was the unlucky one. It decided to let go of the cliff as he was crawling around its outer side. It fell, took him with it, and crushed him to death. It had been a problem. They paused silently. The solution had been to ferry in bus-jacks, by helicopter.

We started the walk up in lovely weather – slightly muggily hot – at eight-thirty the next morning; trudging the usual uneventful walk, up across a splodgy wilderness towards the base of the 'British Alps'. The path followed a river and came quickly to a precarious Amazonian bridge spanning a gushing torrent, deep pools and rapids of stormy blue. I was glad to have James 'Paddy' Stephenson, Sarah Kay and, from last night, Eoghain and his Skye accent with its little tremor of Norse in the Scottish brogue to guide me, as we filed across the bridge, heading up to the magic point where the grass gave way to sheer rock.

Eoghain had the lope of an experienced hill climber. He set a cracking pace, his long strides taking us up the base of the hills, which stood out of the surrounding flats like bubbles of granite. This was the famous gabbro, or 'grabbo' as I kept calling it: a mental reference to its renowned adhesive qualities. Almost any surface can be slippery in wet and ice, but the stone of which the Cuillins are made is like pumice or scored rubber.

It was exhilarating to saunter up the stuff. In dry weather, and it had become a warm, clear morning with a distant fish eagle swimming high in the ether, the lower rock almost challenges you to walk vertical slopes – satisfactorily flattening out at the top of each giant boulder so you can jump on and up to the next. And Eoghain was always pressing on ahead.

He paused and turned. I joined him and he pointed at the green sea of land below us. Unbroken by fences, it wallowed away to an estuary on the western edge of the island, some ten miles away. We could already see the sunny twinkle of Portree, far beyond the intrusive geometric blocks of Forestry Commission plantations. Beyond, over Raasay, to the north-east, the peaks of the western shore marched back towards Sutherland, where I had started.

'See there.' He pointed down to a speck of white. 'That's a little rented cottage.' He swivelled round and pointed the other way. 'There used to be a high farm round the side of the mountain to the east there. It was a hard life. But there's nobody there now.'

We rested and ate by a tarn in a giant natural amphitheatre where, like visitors to a theatre, we veered between whispers and shouts, to test the echoes. The base of the next, much steeper stage up to the peaks was now almost directly above us. Pinnacles and teeth of rock were sticking out of long skirts of broken stone. We were at the eastern edge of the Cuillins.

Eoghain marked them off until he came to 'Chinaman's Gully'.

Paddy stopped him. 'Why that name?'

RIGHT: The Abbey Road of the Western Isles.

Eoghain looked a little guilty. 'It's because of the Chinaman who fell there.'

I had begun to learn that mountain climbing was more often about stamina and covering distance than acrobatic feats. The scree slope was a lateral traipse across the side of the mountain. For twenty minutes, perhaps longer, we picked our way upwards and sideways over a giant's rock garden and then paused to look back. While moving, it is impossible to gaze around. The path is too ragged. But now with the pinnacles revealing their true character as crumbling, elevated, looming stumps immediately above us and the ridge soaring away on the other side of the cleft we were negotiating, we stopped and let the air of this place fold around us.

Two ravens took off from the crag somewhere in the slight streaks of mist around the top of Am Basteir and bounced across the void, above our heads.

'See there,' said Paddy. 'They're turning on to their backs.'

Like relaxed swimmers doing a bit of backstroke for a change, the ravens rolled and flew languidly upside down.

'I've heard that they are the only birds that do that. It's for pleasure, I am sure.'

Who was to know? But I envied their extra mobility. It felt sometimes as if the only possible response would have been to try to take off oneself. The wheeling ravens mock earthbound plodding climbers, with our feeble, crawling 'challenges' and 'conquests'.

We could still see the hotel, and now, very clearly, beaming in the sunlight the smooth cone of the first of the Red Cuillins beyond – a mere bun compared with our family loaf but 2000 feet from top to bottom. Paddy had run up and down it in the annual race only last year. The record was an hour, and the first recorded run had been undertaken by the Sepoy servant of a visiting climber. He had done it, that first run, in an hour and twenty.

'And in bare feet too,' said Paddy ruefully.

Eoghain had turned and was pointing up to the ridge above. 'Can you see? Look there's someone coming down now.'

For a while I couldn't. But Eoghain directed me where to look along the jagged crest and I spotted him, impossibly tiny, a little black bug, crawling down the jagged outline, and instantly making the pinnacles much huger than I had imagined.

'He's probably doing the ridge from end to end,' said Eoghain. 'Robert, who is

LEFT: After the rain on the Cuillins.

a mountain guide, has done the whole route in seven hours, but it's best to allow longer.'

We were heading up to cross routes with the bug. Our destination would be on the back of the caterpillar of the Cuillins itself, at a point where it looped down, another half an hour ahead. We passed three others scrabbling towards us – two young blokes and an older man, dressed for a nightclub in leather jackets and motorcycle boots. One of them wore a mid-length car coat. And absurdly, on this slew of a 500-acre slope, we had to stand to one side like guests at a cocktail party to let them pass.

We plugged on. I caught Eoghain's eye.

'Oh, you meet all sorts on a mountain,' he said.

And finally the ridge itself. And I understood more clearly where I was. We hit the pitch of the roof at one of its lower points but it was still a peak. The slope fell away on the other side to a chaos of broken, sweeping cliffs, falling down to the sea. Looking south across towards Rum and Eigg, I could see that we were at the beginning of a crest. It swooped and jiggered down to join us from startling broken pinnacles to the east, and swooped and jiggered on, up and away from us, twisting along for miles, to encompass a vast, black, seemingly unscalable wall, to the west and south. This was the black fortress that I had seen above me from the rowing boat. That nickel blot was the upper loch I had walked along. After all my fussing about danger, I wanted to be the climber we had seen earlier and do the lot. We went a short distance further, clambering and slithering over gigantic shards of broken granite, up and down the undulations of the heap, until we reached, completely incongruously, just as we had on Ben Hope, a concrete trig point at the summit of Bruach na Frithe.

Some of the romantic poets in the late eighteenth century, when mountain climbing was a new experience, or at least a new experience for writers, climbed peaks and expected more excitement. They had wanted something transcendent – a powerful rush of emotion. They experienced, exactly as I did now on this pinnacle, their own clumsiness. It was just like ordinary walking about. It wasn't special walking about. The body was still tied to the ground. It wasn't a different physical experience. They had to content themselves with their own lumpiness and gaze around in awe, and so did we.

ABOVE: The summit of the caterpillar.
BELOW: Sarah, Paddy, Eoghain and Griff hold on to a trig point.

We were very lucky. It was still spectacularly clear. There were enough boiling, steamy clouds around the far tips of the Black Cuillins to provide the essential weather drama.

'Would you buy it then, Eoghain, if you had the cash?'

Eoghain didn't really think for a moment. 'Oh no.' He was amused by the idea. 'He only wants the money for his castle. Who's going to pay for something that is part of the island?'

Eoghain owned the place already. He wasn't going to fork out for it, even if he had the money. We turned to go. And began the long clamber down.

We were soon off the rocks and bounding over the tussocks cut by streams and littered with boggy patches. At one point I used a bright-green patch as a stepping stone. It bounced soggily beneath my foot, but I jumped on and up to the bank.

ABOVE: Just ordinary sitting about at 2000 feet.

'Well, you were lucky there,' said Eoghain. 'That's a boiggish.' He spent some time trying to think of the translation of the Gaelic and settled on 'doom hole'. The green mat was caused by plants drinking the fresh water bubbling up from a spring. I had been lucky it had supported me at all. Usually there was a water-filled chasm underneath and the unwary disappeared with a ploosh.

I felt that Eoghain should probably come with me on any further adventures, to protect me. But I had been lucky and I was quite spry too. Perhaps I was getting fitter myself. I decided I could take a night on the town.

That evening I waited for Janice, Stacey, Gael and Will on the corner of Portree Square. They had offered to show me Skye at night. It was quiet so I chatted to the bloke in the burger lorry. He was from Maryland in the States. 'You should come on later at about eleven,' he said. 'There are big men out of the pubs and they like a fight to round off the evening.'

They are indeed big men on Skye. Even the little boys bicycling round the square in the dark were big. One wanted to tell me about the mountains. 'You'll have do the Cuillins,' he advised me. 'I tried. I got halfway up.' Others were skateboarding out into the road to prove how tough they were. The streets echoed with the roar of souped-up Escorts.

'That's what the boys do,' Janice said when they joined me. 'They buy cars and fit extra bits on them.'

'Some of the girls too, these days,' Stacey added. Stacey was training to be a sports physio. She was back for the weekend from Glasgow. 'Really, just to be in the film,' she explained.

The pub we were off to, the Tongadale, was a 'cosy one'. There was a convention of coastguards in town, but the three guys leaning on the table made from a ship's tabernacle all ran local boats. They wanted to take me out to see the fish eagle, but I explained that I was busy going up mountains, and tonight to a ceilidh, to get a flavour of what life was like in the wild outlying Highland islands.

There were more big men at the dance itself – fifty-year-olds in good trousers and well-pressed shirts. A couple of people wore kilts. It was taking place in the old seamen's hall – with a stone rope carving round the door and a high, beamed roof on the inside. And the people in it were ordinary Skye people, of all ages – quite a lot of grannies and girls in groups and boys with pimples and too much stuff in their hair, plus a smattering of red, weather-beaten faces. In a town without a decent CD shop the ceilidh was still a major entertainment.

'Everybody goes to a ceilidh. It's not just for the tourists,' Janice told me.

There weren't any tourists there, but there were some incomers, including a man who gave up his job with Volkswagen to open a shop selling those exhausts we had heard in the street. He was doing good business. But the girls told me they had to take a trip to Inverness, or a weekend in Glasgow, if they wanted to go shopping properly.

People were already dancing and the band was a no-nonsense, rattling hoot. It was led by a shaven-headed accordionist, in black, with the belly and the shoulders on him too, raising the tempo every time, so that even if you weren't dancing you had to tap your toes. And the fishermen and the divers of a certain age were up and urging me on. 'Get up and dance, Griff,' they shouted.

People grabbed me and took me up on the parquet floor, where I somehow remembered I could do the Gay Gordons. And after that Janice showed me how to do another dance – two forward, two back, two side to side and then a twirl for eight beats – pretty simple. In a while I could start to add a little flourish to the forward step – just hit it with a little toe tap. It was exhausting stuff.

For Strip the Willow we formed up into a line – so many wanting to take part that there was hardly room to accommodate them. Sharon came across and she wasn't gentle with me at all. We had to start at the end up by the band, who were sawing and fingering out a blasting beat and Sharon swung me round with centrifugal force, and I was off down the line, linking arms with each of the women in turn, then back to Sharon and on, grabbing at the line again – young women, little girls, mums and matrons all twirled me and threw me back. I tried to slow when I came to a wiry-looking granny with a tight, black perm but I misjudged her. She got her bony elbow under mine and seized me with a fierce grip and swung me round so firmly that my head reeled.

And it reels still. Incomer, outgoer, open to all or privately owned, the cold far north of Scotland may increasingly need tourists to make a living, but it still feels like a different place, a separate region. And I was beginning to like these hilly places.

ABOVE: The joy of emptiness. Sarah, Paddy and Eoghain contemplate the view.

CENTRAL SCOTLAND

CHAPTER TWO

Central Scotland

'Oh, you're going up the Ben … Yuh.' The dreadlocked shop assistant measuring my feet looked up and nodded. Apparently Cameron McNeish had written up our recent shared adventure in *Modern Mountaineering* or *Tight Trousers and Big Pack Magazine* (actually *The Great Outdoors*). We were climbing news.

But I was trying to buy a pair of running shoes and I was being unhelpfully vague. Dave wanted to know the exact and precise nature of my proposed mountain activity. As I now know, mountain gear, from the underpants out, is created only after strenuous and dedicated research – particularly, as far as I could see, into the exact type of waffle for the brochure.

I needed 'an ankle-supporting yet flexible lightweight shoe with cushioned sole and advanced breathability'. So I got one. In fact I got two. Now I was equipped to run up a mountain.

A week later I put on my new plimsolls and walked out to greet what I was told was an unusual sight in Fort William. For once, the most iconic of mountains, the nation's favourite landmark, the highest mountain in Britain, Ben Nevis, rose up from Loch Linnhe without a veil of fog to hide its gargantuan-ness. I could see the whole thing from top to toe.

This great green loaf is the Trafalgar Square of mountains. It is a destination wilderness. There is a well-trodden route to the top. When I mentioned to a friend that I was off to climb it she was unimpressed. 'I pushed a baby buggy up there once,' she said. I lacked an infant but I was prepared to try a challenge of my own.

Later that day I negotiated a path through a herd of sheep, trotting up the road

ABOVE: Fully equipped with the right brochure waffle.

to the gate by the shed-like but enormous café at the base, to meet up with three women who were training for the Ben Nevis run.

It was May. It was cold. I got my trousers off and started joking with Morag Aitken about heart attacks and drugs, while Emmy and Nicky Donaldson watched and stretched. They were sisters. As we stood by the gate stripping down to running kit, their father, a park ranger, came by.

I thought he looked at me oddly. 'You'll be sticking to the path,' he said pointedly.

I nodded and looked haplessly at the others. They were nodding too, rather more vigorously than me. This was because we weren't going to stick to the path at all. We were going up to the 'halfway lochan'; some enormous pond in a cruck in the hill. The tourist path gently snakes its way there, but a true runner cuts the loops and, at key points, heads straight up, ignoring all the park rangers and the risk of erosion. And this is what we were secretly planning. He walked off and I began to wonder what I was up to.

I run. I blunder around Regent's Park a few times a week. There is an imperceptible incline on part of it. But secretly I had recently been training – pushing a little harder, making sure I ran when I didn't feel it was strictly necessary and looking out for hills to try out my thighs on. But it was now getting tense. We had to wait while a cameraman went on ahead of us. My stubby legs were trembling.

Morag, Emmy and Nicky had begun by standing at the finishing line to welcome their men back. Then they decided to have a go themselves. In fact in the case of the Donaldson sisters it was their dad, the park ranger, who started it. And while we waited they showed me a photograph of their mother and father, embracing at the end of a run some twenty years before. Mum had decided to join Dad. It became a family business. It was such a sexy picture. But it was a sexy thing. Men and women urged each other on. They met on the slopes. They nursed each other's injuries and exulted in each other's triumphs. I hoped I was ready for that. And finally, off we went. A little uphill, but nothing extreme.

'Slow down, slow down!' Morag was gesticulating. 'You'll use up all your puff.'

So I slowed, like men slow: with a little extra spring to demonstrate my reserves. In truth, I felt like some aged donkey given three rather beautiful fillies to urge him

LEFT: The mountain of dread, Ben Nevis, looking a push-over.

on. Helpfully, they took it in turns to run in front. But within minutes I couldn't care what was ahead, I cared only that it was all upwards, upwards, upwards. And sometimes, even worse, sideways.

There's an extra element to hill running that you don't get on the flat: it's the constant decision-making. The path ahead is a crazy, paved, stepping-stone ascent – a little leap on to one rock, a spring up to the next. Running under these conditions you are constantly making judgements. But this is the easy stage.

Running down, the choices become gambles. Suddenly the force of gravity is with you. 'Horrendous things happen,' Emmy told me. 'I've seen men miss their step and turn a complete somersault before they get a foot on the rock again.'

'It's a miracle more aren't hurt,' Nicky shouted.

'But plenty are. They break legs, gash shoulders, smash their skulls…'

ABOVE: 'Haf, hoof, ha, ha, oof, ha foo.' Morag comforts the broken nag.

I was barely listening. And I couldn't have answered anyway. I would have been happy to risk the somersaults to be bounding downwards now, instead of heaving my twelve stone upwards, with every effortful step.

'You don't really run up the steep bits,' Emmy was reassuring me. 'It's more a quick walk.'

Yes, but she was very quick, like a speeded-up toy, pounding rhythmically upwards from rock to rock with a steady mechanical pulse which I couldn't match. And I wasn't really running any more. I wasn't really sure if I was walking either. I was willing myself to stick my feet on, and pump my thighs up, but I wasn't conscious of it.

And then we left the path and cut the first corner, leaving the steady rocky incline and heading straight up a steep, grassy cliff.

My breath was rasping through my lungs. Just trying to get enough oxygen into my body to enable the system to move onwards was becoming impossible. We had to get to the lochan in under an hour. Usually I ran for twenty minutes and rested for the remainder of the evening. And that was on the flat. I thought back to the week before, when I imagined I had misheard Allan MacRae. We were standing half up to our ankles in cow dung feeding his Highland cattle. He told me casually that he used to run up Ben Nevis in his younger days. I had no idea then that such a barmy race even existed. It started in 1895, for men only. Women joined in 1930. The leading racers now got up and down again in just about an hour and a half – a crazy time.

But when Allan talked about it, just that casual mention, he made me wonder what it would be like. This is the competitive absurdity that energizes most mountain sport. I wanted to have a crack. Me! There are foot races these days over just about every lump, bump and hillock in the world.

But it was lovely going with girls. They were honestly solicitous not challengingly solicitous. They didn't say things like, 'Are you all right – can you manage this?' like a man would have done. They said things like, 'Oh, you're doing well,' and, 'You've done this before,' like a mum (even when I was clearly being overtaken by determined walkers). After twenty minutes we finally passed one camera. Was I even going upwards? Was I actually in motion or just convulsing like an electrified fish? My shorts weighed as heavily as a suit of armour.

Nicky, the champion, forged on. I twitched after her. The other two trailed a little. The last section seemed absurd. The path had curved way to the west. We were mounting a sharp bank – a short cut – that just went on and on and on, up grass and through an absorbent kitchen scourer drenched with hill water. It seemed an act of will to order myself to continue. One massive ham flopped up after another. Hill runner? I was moving at the pace of an old woman with a broken stairlift.

After another half hour, on a bare and insignificant tawny stretch of path, we finally got there. I stopped. I ceased to move forward, and just spasmed. It was time for a witticism. I stood, crouching slightly forward, trying to gulp enough air into my lungs in order to do something more than raucously honk for a minute.

'I once…' I finally began '…went pony trekking in Montana … ha, ha, hahh … and when the horse hit the first hill it … euuch, honk, honk … started… Arrrrrgh … puffing … oof … ha … and wheezing and… Arrrr … groaning … and made me feel … arrr … terrible.'

Morag had her stopwatch out. 'Forty-eight minutes,' she said.

If I wanted to qualify for the proper race, I had to make it to this point in under an hour. I had won that privilege.

But I had cheated. I didn't tell the girls as I accepted their congratulations but I had actually donated every joule of energy to getting to where I was. Nothing could have induced me to run on further. Not even the sight of the three of them beckoning me on like wild maidens in a Norse saga. They jagged on and away into the rapidly thickening mist to complete their training, but I was done.

As I changed my socks and wrestled with the laces of my walking boots, designed on principles abandoned by corset makers over a hundred years ago, a constant stream of revellers hiked up the mountain path behind me. Perhaps it was 'the Ben', as the man in the London shop was keen to call it, as if Ben Nevis were a personal mate. The walkers seemed excited. They reminded me of a queue of Saturday-night ticket holders for a hit show in the West End. They had their passes for the attraction and it was geeing them up. Two determined, slight men with premature baldness (runners) were threading their way through the queue. I hailed them (as only a fellow runner could).

'We're doing the Three Peaks,' one of them gasped.

RIGHT: It was April but the snow still covered the higher slopes of the Ben.

Not just half of one massive mountain, then, but three in succession.

A number of the parties trudging up were indeed parties. The mixed group of men and women in fleeces were from a fire service and they were climbing for charity. And they were nothing to do with the three or four guys who were rolling a barrel up the slope as part of some wedding stunt. A few weeks before I arrived someone had discovered the remains of a piano near the top. It had been carried up as a bet and then abandoned. A car had once been driven up here as well. Nevis was a dork magnet. It was on the fun-run list. It was a stag-night favourite.

The guidebooks say that Nevis translates as 'Mountain of Heaven'. But philologists demur. Nobody knows exactly what the name means, but it's more likely to be a derivative of 'dread' or 'fearful'. As the red-faced boys heaved their barrel past me, I was sure they were sublimely unaware that the place had once been so off the map, so out of public consciousness, that no one ever regularly climbed it.

There was a legend that, when the snows no longer shone from the peak, the Campbells would no longer own the land. At some point in the Middle Ages when they were having rather wonderful summers, the Campbells sent men to the top of the mountain to lay straw on the snow, just to be sure, but that was sometime in the fourteenth century. Otherwise nobody really disturbed the place until the botanists arrived, followed by the geologists and then the weathermen.

The path I was sitting next to had originally been marked out by a man on a pony, called Clement Wragge. In 1881 Clement volunteered to climb to the top of the mountain every day. He took his Newfoundland dog, Renzo, with him and recorded the weather conditions from June to October. He was quickly dubbed 'Inclement' Wragge by the locals. But he persevered, and sent his observations back to the Scottish Meteorological Society in Edinburgh.

As for me, I was dressed just in time. With a ferocious abruptness a cloud romped in. It is said that you can experience all the seasons in a single afternoon on Ben Nevis. The wind barrelled into me. I have to admit my first reaction was one of comical amazement. I could hardly stand. Marjory Roy, a meteorologist and historian of weather forecasting, who had come to meet me and was going to show me the weather station on the top of the mountain, mocked my astonishment. 'Oh, this is just a little breeze,' she said. She had a yellow plastic doobrie, like one

ABOVE: All the seasons in a single day – including a monsoon.
BELOW: The summit of Ben Nevis as I never experienced it.

of those puffers asthmatics use, and held it up to the storm. 'About seventy miles an hour,' she announced.

The rain was bouncing off her spectacles like hail on a car windscreen. We tried to find an outcrop of rock to shelter us so that we could hold a hurriedly shouted conversation. The original plan had been to go on up, a further 1000 feet, to the summit, to examine the ruins of the weather station, she with her geographer's hat on, me with my *Restoration* hat on, but we decided to abandon our expedition. Hats were long gone.

Over on the path, a few men and women in jeans and pullies were hurrying down ahead of us. They should have been wearing more than shocked expressions. The guidebook, or Dave in the shop, would have told them that. The racket was intolerable, but, of course, here in late May, it was nothing compared with the conditions encountered by the personnel in the weather hut. The meteorologists bunked down up there as if it were an Arctic station. Sometimes it looked like an Arctic station. Photographs show their hut submerged beneath pillars of heaped snow. Only their wind-measuring pole indicated that they were there at all. And they had to climb up that to shake the snow off it.

Despite being partly funded by Queen Victoria herself, who no doubt shared her subjects' fascination with the climate, the weather station was not a huge success. It sent its measurements to the Meteorological Society to be analysed, by way of the electric telegram, but the belief that the extra height would add omniscience to weather analysis was misplaced. Mountain weather was too freakish. Lowland Scots wetness was formulated far out in the Atlantic. Weather stations out in the Hebrides were much more accurate. Marjory had recently discovered all the painstakingly dutiful records, bundled away in the archives, largely unopened, and unread or acted upon.

As early as 1904 the enterprise was called off. The stone shed was abandoned. The place was turned into an equally unsuccessful temperance hotel. If no one wanted information from the top of the highest peak, fewer still wanted a night up there without the consolation of a dram or two. It has since fallen down.

Still, I was sorry to turn and go down the mountain, but did so with my respect for Mr Wragge heightened. He would have carried on. Or, at least, he would have done until they finally built that brand-new station at the top. He was turned

down for the post of chief inspector after all that voluntary daily service. He left in a huff for Australia. Only his pony track survives.

Early scientists were fascinated by the mountains. Botanists hung from cliffs looking for new plants. (It was a botanist who officially claimed the first ascent of Ben Nevis.) Geologists started chipping bits off, looking for metal. Geographers carted barometers up scree falls to measure the pressure. In the early nineteenth century it was considered terrifically bad form to climb a mountain without scientific equipment. Adventurers in the Alps were urged to borrow barometers for propriety's sake. But here in Scotland they arrived in the eighteenth century, after a deliberate policy had been formulated, at the highest levels, to tame the Highlands.

From where I was, looking out and down, I might have commanded a grand panorama of that story – but the mist, the driving rain and the low-flying cloud

ABOVE: When the wind gets up to 70 mph I do an impression of Albert Steptoe.

meant that the view had to remain imaginary. I had to take it for granted that below me and away to the south stretched the network of highways that had first opened up the wild roof of Britain.

Ah yes. What a joy it is to drive in the Highlands. The sweeping curves, the snaking carriageways, the soaring gradients. No wonder Men and Motors send their men and their motors up this way to practise being manly by excessive motoring. I whisked south in a handy, gas-guzzling behemoth.

The roads are miracles of design and ingenuity. It's no surprise that one of Scotland's greatest exports is engineering. The outlying towns were finally reached via daring bridges, vast cuttings and gigantic defiles. They taxed the skills of generations of Stephensons, Rennies and Telfords. But originally the roads were built by soldiers, for soldiers.

In the eighteenth century the lowland areas of Britain had made a forced march towards civilization. Communications had improved, the commonality of wealth had extended. The feudal systems of loyalty and servitude had been abandoned. A big Protestant, people's king had been appointed and he worked with parliament and commerce, supporting and supported by the Anglican Church. In the north the Scottish Enlightenment, based in Edinburgh and

Glasgow, led the world in civilized thinking.

That civilized world, however, ended at the foot of the mountains. Up in the wilderness a different Scottish order persevered. The Highlands were a part of the United Kingdom where the reach of the law was physically limited. Commerce didn't go on there and people were attached to their tribes before their government, which was miles away, anyway, over a boggy, rocky wasteland, in England.

There were two great Scottish rebellions in the seventeen hundreds, known as 'the '15' and 'the '45', after the years in which they occurred. Both came out of the mountains. By then the government of the United Kingdom had decided they wanted to win the hearts and minds of an unwilling population, so they set out to break a few skulls.

Lacking armoured cars, eighteenth-century generals needed to march their troops swiftly about the Highlands in order to police what was a wild, boggy, impenetrable, uncharted landscape, 'for its own good'. And to do this, they needed roads, like the one I was travelling south on now.

The pass through the Great Glen is justly famous. I pulled my car over with incredible difficulty, slewing out of the onward rush of traffic just before the twisty bit that wriggles through the top.

Beyond my lay-by was a chunk of wall and an old track. Along the grassy sections, patches of flat cobbles broke through. The embankment was shored up with carefully constructed stone walling. This was the best place to look at the remains of the original pathway. Most of General Wade's route is buried deep beneath the modern highway, but I was able to get down on my hands and knees and look at the original high road to the Highlands, made without the benefit of JCBs and bulldozers. Then I rolled over and looked up at the cliffs.

The Redcoats who built the road were divided into two groups. One unit worked on the roadway, digging and shovelling. Another positioned itself in the rocks above. They were keeping guard, in case the wild and hairy men descended from the heights – the preferred way of overwhelming invaders ever since the Picts had charged out of the mist.

As it happened, the guards envied the shovellers because the workers were paid more, but eventually Wade and his successors built 1100 miles of roads into the mountain regions. Soon soldiers could zoom from stronghold to stronghold.

LEFT: The road to the Highlands has a speed limit.

Properly, the Highlands were remote no more. The Hanoverians were suitably grateful. There is even a sixth verse to the National Anthem:

Lord grant that Marshal Wade
May by thy mighty aid
Victory bring.
May he sedition hush,
And like a torrent rush,
Rebellious Scots to crush.
God save the Queen!

It's not much sung these days, particularly perhaps in Scotland. Hibernian patriots can take comfort, though, that the roads were indeed used to ferry troops, quickly, effectively and devastatingly, by Charles Stuart, Bonnie Prince Charlie, the last great Highland rebel. But he was defeated, and as every Scottish schoolboy knows, the clans were hammered as a result. But it was a long and bloody process.

The next morning I got in a work boat, reeking as work boats do of fish and rope, and motored down the Kyle of Leven under startling clouds. Can grey be lurid? These were huge and heavy and densely bluish. An island ahead shone like a livid green gash in the water.

Eilean Munde is known as 'the Island of the Dead' with good reason. As we came around the northern side I could see that the long grass was broken by slabs of upright granite. It was an ancient graveyard. The victims of the infamous Glencoe Massacre in 1692 were buried here, alongside the remains of their ancestors and forebears.

It cannot have been easy to get a coffin ashore. There was no funeral jetty. The boat bumped up against the bladderwrack and I slithered on to the granite rocks as best I could, as Stuart Nicol, a local guide and historian, led me on, up a sandy bank. The base was littered with discarded blue eggshells and broken mussels. So few people came here, otters felt happy to feast on these rocks.

'The murderers broke the cardinal rules of the Highlands,' Stuart explained. The soldiers had been billeted on the MacDonalds, and taken in with due hospitality. 'Even your bitterest enemy was to be given a roof over his head and food at the table.'

ABOVE: Stuart Nicol escorts me to the island of the dead.
BELOW: The top of the Great Glen. The remains of Wade's road can be seen to the right.

'Like a Bedouin or Apache,' I ventured.

Stuart got quite excited. 'In fact when the clans were forced into exile many left for America. Several Highland chieftains confronted Native American chieftains. They took one look at each other and established an instant rapport. The stance, the garb – it was all familiar.'

We came to the monument. The soldiers, who were not, it should be emphasized, English soldiers but Scottish Lowlanders, stayed for twelve days with the MacDonalds. Their commander received orders that he was to kill the entire male line. No MacDonald under seventy was to be spared. Some of the soldiers were disgusted by what they were asked to do. One found a child hiding under a bridge and refused to kill him, telling his commander that it was a dog. But the majority carried out their orders. And like all ghastly reprisals, like all repressions and acts of extreme violence by central government, the stain, seemingly, can never

ABOVE: The Fort William versus Newtonmore shinty match.

be washed away. Stuart and I stood by the granite monument and great thunder clouds towered above us.

After the ultimate English victory (or the victory of the lowlands as perhaps we should see it) some fifty years later, the clans were proscribed and everything to do with them was suppressed. The Gaelic language, the system of fealty, the tartan dress; anything that differentiated mountain life was outlawed.

The following day I turned off the road past Newtonmore on to a bumpy track and parked up with the other 4 x 4s. The sports field was just north of the town. It was blustery. As I got out of the car I was happy to pull my anorak up around my ears, adjust my muffler and hunch my shoulders forward in the familiar stance of the padded-up spectator at a local derby. It was bracing. The players' legs were frozen red. The sky was thick with high, blown cloud.

Two teams were out – bright yellow and hooped blue and white. These last were Newtonmore, the home team. But it was Fort William, the canaries, who were favoured. The consensus seemed to be that Newtonmore could hope for little more than a bloody nose. Bloody noses were quite common; bloody foreheads too, and bloody lips and ears as well, so I was told.

From a distance shinty may resemble hockey – but nobody was wearing a short, blue, pleated skirt. The sticks were bevel-edged and rarely held discreetly below knee level. The solid-looking white ball went arcing through the air.

'Get it there, Davy! Slog it, man! Oh, good hit.' Along the stoop, the women of Newtonmore bellowed support.

Luckily the principles of shinty are easy enough to grasp even for a Sassenach. There is a smallish goal at each end of a huge field and a large body of tough-looking men to knock the ball into them. They do this with those sticks and they happily barge each other out of the way to get at the ball.

'Ooch.' The crashes had the gutsiness of American football – but the swinging, cracking, head-pulping lashes with the sticks made me flinch and look away. 'They're allowed to raise the sticks up like that, then?'

'Oh yes.' Karen was standing to my left. Her little boy, all three feet of him, was grinning at the game and shouting.

'And don't they sometimes miss the ball and hit each other?'

'Oh yes.'

'Doesn't it worry you? Do you have a relative or friend out there?'

'Oh no, I'm the doctor.'

Karen was a local GP. She was attending the game on a professional basis. Her green bag was behind us in the changing room. 'The difficulty is actually in trying to get them to come off,' she explained. 'They'll be out there with blood running down their faces, unable to see, and carrying on as if nothing had happened.'

'Oof. Ouch!' I was pulling a face at every encounter.

Rushing about in the middle of the mêlée was a man I had come to see – a fierce Highlander with a strapped knee – John Sloggie, the referee.

After the game I went up to John Sloggie's croft on the side of Loch Garry. We sat out on a bench overlooking a kingfisher-blue lake. 'Everybody has to have a game,' he said, with such power that I nodded, rather than admitting that I didn't have any particular game myself. It seemed a good idea to agree with John. He fixed me with a rather uncompromising expression. I was glad I was only trying to interview him rather than argue a point of shinty law.

Like one or two other 'Highland games', shinty seemed to be the sort of thing that started as a trial of strength after closing time. 'I bet I can toss that huge log further than you.' Or 'Let's get a blackthorn stick and hit pebbles.' (Cravenly, I kept this thought to myself.) In 1893 shinty teams had become an association. The game was tamed: the association regularized the rabble and laid out a set of rules, rules which John Sloggie was clearly now sharply keen to enforce.

He took me down to his shed and showed me how the best modern shinty stick was made, by Sloggie himself, building up laminations of oak and hickory, steaming the result, and bending the end over into a curve which was then shaped into a wedge. I tried to stand my ground as John whisked the stick around within a few inches of my head like some ancient master in a martial-arts film demonstrating the magic powers of his craft.

But the reason why John manufactured these sticks was rather more down-to-earth than 'a calling'. He made them to pay his way. He had his own sheep up on communal grazing, he had cattle below the farm, but he was a Highlander as history had made him, driven on to marginal land by the Clearances and now finding it harder and harder to make a living.

RIGHT: John Sloggie fixes me with a referee's glittering eye.

'Diversify, they say. That's what we have to do.'

Through the dusty window of the shed, beyond the bandsaws and the unused baulks of timber, we could see down the glorious loch.

'There were many families down there but they've gone,' John told me. As well as working as a deer factor, he himself had been a postman in the district for years. Shortly after marrying he had gone to sea and earned his certificate of marine engineering. His own children, after walking miles down the valley to get to shinty matches on Saturdays, had gone to find work off the mountains. His life had been one of constant reinvention and enterprise, but he was one of the few. People are still deserting a hard life – though on this wonderful day it was difficult to see why. But mountains are hard masters.

The following day I went back to Fort William, took a side turning, lumbered up through some forestry pine trees and found myself at the back door to Ben Nevis.

Heather Morning was waiting for me. She was an experienced guide and had just spent the past few months carting people off to Antarctica to complete their 8000-metre challenge, climbing in every continent, including, so it seemed, the frozen ones. Now she was going to get me up the north face of the Ben via an ice wall.

This seemed a bit of a leap. So far the only mountain climbing I had attempted had been up the huge snowdrifts of Ben Hope and Suilven. I was pretty convinced that they were far too dangerous for me, so I set about expressing my nervousness in the only proper way for a middle-aged male, by being slightly irritable and a little disparaging.

'I'm not a climber.'

'Never mind.'

'I'm not sure I see the point.'

'I'm not sure there is one.'

We were trudging again. You have to walk to climb and we were following a broad, rushing stream, dipping down to the water and then clambering up a bank. Over to our right, beyond the gurgling torrent, across a level of torpid bog, towered a severe shard of grey cliff. It was a wall. You instantly get why climbers talk of buttresses, cornices, gables and chimneys. They might throw in skirting boards too. You get why Welsh place names give the crests of hills the title of 'castle'. It was as if, on looking in the mirror, you discovered that the pretty green dress of Ben Nevis had no back at all.

'It was a couple of English blokes who came up this side first – the Nicholsons…' Heather told me. She was English herself, from Leeds. 'One day the weather people were startled to look down and see this father-and-son team coming up over the top of the cliff. No announcement or nothing.'

They were lucky they had come up quickly. One route is called Gardez Loo, because the gully had been the station's toilet.

'I suppose that added the extra challenge that you climbers like,' I said.

'Well, these climbs became popular enough after that.'

We had been walking for about an hour and had started to follow the stream up its waterfalls, traversing a mounded, pink, granite lump of rock the size of the National Theatre. The valley was closing in on both sides now. The cliff seemed taller and more menacing than ever. Ahead of us, perched on an outcrop looking down towards a distant Loch Eil, was a splendid mountain hut, built by grieving parents in memory of a young climber who died in the First World War.

Heather bashed around with several massive padlocks and we got inside. She was a member. They kept the amateurs out in the cold. I was privileged. In the

high season you had to book a place, so you could sleep overnight in one of the hard-looking bunks and be ready for your ascent the following day. It was modelled on similar huts in the Alps, with a cooker, a big table and a library of heavily bound visitors' books. No cushions, plenty of soup and a matey bunk-down for all. I was surprised to find that the really busy season was the winter.

'The gullies fill up with ice and that's what they started experimenting with in the forties. It's the biggest draw, because what you get in Scotland is Arctic climate,' Heather explained.

Scotland had been left to one side to begin with, but had grown in stature as the sport progressed. The climbing fraternity went to the Alps, because their primary impetus was conquest. Everybody wanted to be the first to the summit, to tick off another mountain. But once they had got to the top of everything, they looked for

ABOVE: Heather points out my deficiencies.

something new and it was the route itself that became important. Rock climbing is not about getting to the summit so much as having a difficult time doing it.

And then some damn fool thought they would try it frozen. This was a whole new form of climbing. You cut your way up with an axe and crampons and went up vertically – essentially monkeying up a frozen waterfall.

We left the hut and headed straight towards the cliff. Our path took us closer to the face and ahead of us lay a ruin. It was an avalanche, spread across the valley floor like a huge, toppled sugar bowl. There was nothing British about this. I felt as if I had followed Heather on one of her Antarctic trips, gingerly stepping through polygonal blocks of frozen snow, a football pitch in width – dirty, close to, with crushed rock and black scree dragged down by the fall. You couldn't imagine a

ABOVE: The north face of Ben Nevis – not so easy for a baby buggy.

hapless mountaineer digging himself out of this heavy, clumsy mess. It wasn't a good sign. And we were, after another hour of scrambling, nearing the start point of our proper climb, entering into a Wagnerian amphitheatre. There were no party kegs of beer here, just blackened cliffs on three sides, cut with furrows and chasms, rising up to invisible heights and streaked, every now and again, by great chutes of frozen snow, which were, alas for our ambitions, creaking and dripping and slithering.

'We're too late, I fear,' Heather said.

Unfortunately, it had been a lovely day in this late spring. The sun had shone for most of the afternoon. Winter had had it. Even in this shadowy ice box the season had passed its best.

'I don't think we can risk it.' She pointed up at the crest of a gully where a great crown of ice was ponderously dislodging itself. Water was freely trickling down the nearest snow slope.

I am pretty sure that Heather would have gone on had she been alone, but conditions were wrong for a scornful complete novice to attempt his first ice climb. I didn't mind particularly. Not for the reasons you might imagine. Somehow, having got this far, as usual the interior drive to go on, to stretch myself, was working perfectly. But I was happy to have got to where I had. I can think of nowhere in Britain that had ever matched this looming enclosure for drama and majesty.

I would have to come back. This was my second failed attempt on the summit.

If the original historic impulse had been to cow rebellion in the mountains, the next stage in the taming of the Highlands was to try to bring prosperity via commerce and trade. The shaggy, backward Highland chieftains had been urged to send their sons away to public school. Many of the young men returned with new ideas. They started exploiting their estates in advanced and modern ways. For some this meant making space for more sheep, initiating the ruthless horror of the Highland Clearances. Others would try floating their forests downriver to sell as masts for ships. The more recalcitrant lairds were bullied by forward-thinking committees into projects like the extraordinary Caledonian Canal, a triumph of doomed optimism.

I got a taste of this enterprising project just north of Fort William, where the cut begins its miraculous journey from sea level and joins up with the deep, deep lochs that nestle in the massive geological fault splitting the north in two. A fifty-ton traditional wooden herring drifter, the *Eala Bhan*, was making its ponderous way through a ladder of nine locks, helped by Ted and Toni the lock keepers, steered by Iain MacKay its captain and watched from a comfortable saloon by ten or so elderly American passengers. It was climbing past a dignified small house with a curved bay at the front.

'The cottage was built like that so that Telford could look up and down the canal at the work as it progressed,' Ian told me. He looked ahead. 'Sometimes they were blasting their way through solid rock and other times trying to keep the canal afloat in the bog, lining the sides with Harris tweed to keep the water in.'

The canal was built partly to allow sea-going sailing traffic to avoid having to go into the storm-tossed Minch and up above the bonnet of Scotland, but also to bring prosperity to the mountainous regions themselves. For a start it offered employment to the Highlander, dispossessed of his warrior status and turned off his land to make way for sheep. But Mr Telford and his lieutenants were disappointed by the locals' lack of application. Paid work for other masters was a new concept in the mountains. The workforce tended to wander away at harvest time. They were going to need a complete re-education if the Highlands were ever to be worthy of these great engineering feats; except that the great engineering feats were never quite worthy of the Highlands.

The poet Southey went into raptures over the canal, like Clive James swooning over Concorde, but just like Concorde the whole project was a form of science fiction made real. Yes, boats could cross Scotland, but canal boats found the conditions in the long lochs too rough, and sea boats got too big to squeeze through. It had a brief flourish of usefulness during the Napoleonic Wars, but it never really ignited the Highland economy. Like Concorde, this early attempt at civilization is a tourist attraction now.

The canal wasn't a solitary enterprise. There were other ventures still in use. I headed on and south to Rannoch Moor: an exhilarating wilderness. Today we can admire it for continuing to exist – fifty square miles of emptiness in our standing-room-only society. To the Victorians it was a challenge. As Queen Victoria settled

into her period of listless, inactive mourning, her subjects perpetuated her hyperactive dead husband's legacy by building, bridging and traversing everything in sight.

One morning in January 1889 seven members of the West Highland Line company arrived at the edge of this howling wasteland to walk the route of their new railway to the remote western islands. They were wearing street clothes, had no equipment except umbrellas and got hopelessly lost, but their chairman rallied their spirits and marched them on to safety. They were lucky. The following day the moor was buried in a blizzard which would have killed them all.

As I clambered aboard the northbound train at Rannoch Station, the passengers who had trundled through the night from King's Cross were just getting up. I got a cup of tea from Reg, the steward, and we rattled over another Highland engineering feat. The line to Fort William had had to be laid on rafts of wood, rubble and earth to stop it sinking into the bog. It took seven years to build.

Again, it was a commercial enterprise, driven by fantasies of trade, which were never to take off. Luckily the process of taming the wilderness had had an unforeseen consequence. During the course of the nineteenth century the damp,

ABOVE: The *Eala Bhan* rises through Thomas Telford's ladder of locks at the western end of the Caledonian Canal.

foggy, bleak, uncongenial, impractical and cold Highlands were to become the most fashionable place in the world to build a holiday home.

Travelling for pleasure is a relatively modern invention. One of the earliest tourists in Scotland, Mrs Murray, recommended taking a full set of cutlery and a spare set of carriage springs. Doctor Johnson walked, so he had plenty of time to rehearse his complaints about the accommodation, the scenery and the weather. Neither of these eighteenth-century tourists would have recognized the tartan shortbread wrapper on my morning snack, or easily understood the significance of the tartan bedspread at my hotel or the tartan waistcoats worn by the waitresses in the Tartan Tattie restaurant. They had travelled before Walter Scott.

It is difficult to imagine a book that had more influence on a tourist trade than *Waverley*. Here was a story, written originally to make money, a cheap adventure, but it changed the whole idea of the Scottish Rebellion and those dreadful clans.

When George IV decided it was time to visit Edinburgh and see his kingdom in the North, his entire notion of Hibernia seemed to derive from Walter Scott's thrilling novels. In fact he asked Scott to organize the proceedings and Scott not only invited all the Highland chieftains, some of whom behaved in a suitably uncivilized fashion, waving swords and shouting, but he also insisted that the polite Lowland aristocracy of Edinburgh dress up in the once-banned tartan too.

The King himself was dressed for the occasion, bursting out of his Highland kit. He wore flesh-coloured stockings. One of the ladies gallantly commented that since they had seen so little of him in the past it was gratifying that they should now see so much. The great tartan explosion was born.

I wasn't going all the way to Fort William with the rest of the sleepers. I got off at a pretty little station, Spean Bridge, went through a picket fence and found Daru Rooke, a social historian, waiting for me in a baby-blue bug-eyed Sprite. An open-topped car was a good introduction to the rigours of a Scottish break. It was pissing down. We drove past the banks of a magnificent stretch of open water, Loch Laggan, experiencing the full power of the climate that had created it. On the other side, perfectly placed in a forest of pine, was a sight familiar to viewers of *Monarch of the Glen*, the magnificent and stirring Ardverikie Castle.

When George IV's successor, Queen Victoria, first came to the Highlands she stayed with Cluny of Ardverikie, one of the last of the great chieftains. He had his

ABOVE: Walter Scott, the inventor of Scottish tourism.
BELOW: Rannoch Station – waiting for the overnight train from King's Cross.

own company of archers. He still held clan gatherings and was treated as divine ruler by his tenants, but he was an anomaly. Like so many of the Highland lairds, he was on his uppers. Forestry schemes and new roads notwithstanding, without the old power structures and heavy taxation the lord could not afford to keep his castle. The one we could see in the distance as we drove along the heavily wooded, three-mile approach, with an umbrella over our heads, was not his anyway. It was completely rebuilt by a cotton magnate from Leeds called Sir John Ramsden.

The estate itself was hardly Highland enough for Ramsden. He planted sweeping forests. It was just a holiday home, but he did it up in Scottish Baronial style, adding Jacobean pepperpot towers, battlements and great doors. It looked ready to receive the Munsters.

But I have to admit it was lovely inside. It had to be, really. The weather in the area was so notoriously damp that Queen Victoria vowed she would never go there again and bought in Balmoral instead. Even she might have been seduced by the facilities put in by Ramsden. The pitch-pine-panelled hall sheltered a massive granite and wrought-metal sarcophagus which was the flamboyant heart of a central heating system to rival Bankside Power Station. Daru and I took off our coats.

ABOVE: While it rains on Ardverikie, Daru Rooke and I play billiards beneath the stuffed stags.

Off the other side of the hallway, a full-size snooker table with legs like bollards was overlooked by hundreds of mounted stags' heads. We sneaked about the sitting rooms filled with pumped-up chintzy sofas and libraries of leather-bound books. The palace had cost Ramsden some £180,000 in the last quarter of the 19th century, because it was constructed in such a wild and inaccessible place.

Later I was to meet a modern laird. He led expeditions in an old trawler to go skiing and mountain climbing through the extreme weather of the fjords in winter. But the appeal of Ardverikie is not arduousness. As a visitor you could spend the afternoon being led off to find one of the estate deer, which you then shot dead. Someone else carried it home while you settled in for your third enormous meal of the day, probably taking care not to scoff too many scones because you had to fit in a fourth, dinner, that night. A lot of us still dream of a life like this. We like to go skiing and relax in the jacuzzi. We don't want to work particularly hard to earn our view. We perhaps feel we've done that already in the office.

This fantasy was certainly the driving force behind the development of the tame, containable Highland experience of the next 100 years. Scallops may still come to London on the Western Highlands train but it is the tourists going the other way that sustain the economy.

At the end of the 1960s there was a change. An unholy alliance between the Duke of Edinburgh, Bob Monkhouse and the House of Fraser decided that the once-wild mountains could do better. Why pretend to be some ancient old dusty Scottish laird? What the Cairngorms needed was a resort. It could become a swinging ski spot. To be fair to the Duke, he only arrived to have a look at the snow in Aviemore in a state of disbelief. But he was impressed. There was a rattly, one-man lift and a piste and lots of lovely, crumbly, soft snow. Why not?

The architect was John Poulson, who was later to disappear in a spectacular blizzard of fraud and political corruption. Alas, he doesn't seem to have been much better at the building business. The hotel cesspits overflowed and polluted the glorious Spey. Whether the marketing genius who had made Butlins such a success was the man to put the shine on Britain's premier ski resort I could not possibly say. But he hired Bob and Engelbert to perform. The lifts were built and some at least were suitably impressed.

Pavel Satny had come from Czechoslovakia to Aviemore. I met him on the balcony of a chalet development just outside the main drag. He was a photographer and unfolded a portfolio of some of his work, nostalgic for the lost technicolour of the seventies.

'This was my biggest hit.' He placed an impressively detailed pair of hairy buttocks in front of me. It was a streaker, skiing down the sunny slopes, taken from behind. 'We made it into a poster and sold it in the shop.'

Pavel had snapped the stars who were shipped in for conferences and his prize assignment was to cover *It's a Knockout*. There they were, the famous team, romping on the slopes. 'It was fun,' sighed Pavel wistfully, and I knew what he meant. I myself had been a giant carrot in Prince Andrew's team at Windsor in *It's a Royal Knockout* in the early eighties.

By the early eighties, though, *It's a Knockout* was a little tarnished and so was Aviemore. 'The trouble was we had two good years of snow but it went into decline,' said Pavel.

Two years was hardly enough to build an empire of sophistication in the Cairngorms. It looked to me that Aviemore had survived, but only just. It wasn't really big enough to have become a gold-plated garage forecourt in the sky, like a proper Alpine resort. It shared its Butlins origins with seaside towns, now in the grip of retrograde authorities demanding money and grants to push them into the 1970s, but there was not much that anybody could do if the snow wouldn't come.

That lack of snow at Aviemore could be a problem for Alan Stewart. He is a diver. He has worked every summer, changing anodes on the legs of oil rigs in the North Sea, in order to bring dog sledding home to the Cairngorms. The local laird gave him a sliver of land beyond the town boundaries to house his business.

As I walked up to it, through brilliant late-spring sunshine, along a dirt track and past the regimented stands of Douglas fir, a cacophonous, Walt Disney, *1001 Dalmatians* clamour rose up from a group of sheds ahead, where a clutch of ragged vehicles was strewn across the dirt. Alan had served in the SAS, but he looked a worried man, especially considering he was surrounded by so much unconditional adoration from his dogs. It was April, but unseasonably hot. There was not a scrap of snow to be seen. These were not ideal conditions.

RIGHT: Up to a plateau the size of central London by elevated tram.

As we entered the compound ten or eleven hyperactive mutts began pacing around their enclosures – running out to take a look, jangling their chains, barking a greeting. These dogs would pull their sledge, even if they killed themselves doing it, and, with the sun up and blazing, that's exactly what Alan was worried about.

'It was a Scot who first developed the sport of dog racing – a postman called Alec "Scotty" Allen in fact,' Alan told me. 'Apparently he wanted to find out which of his children had the fastest dogs.' I couldn't hear quite what Alan was saying. The barking was growing louder and louder. I contented myself with nodding, pricking my ears and occasionally licking Alan's face, like every other living thing in the compound.

The huskies certainly managed to soften the heart of this self-respecting, middle-aged, dog-lover daddy. If you think your dog gets thrilled by its daily walkies, then step aside. This was runnies. Better than that, even. It was pullies.

ABOVE: Huskies returning to camp.

These dogs took you for a walk, in a little trolley.

Quite a big trolley really, so it proved. It was a long, lean, cantilevered soap-box cart with wire wheels. I would have loved to have taken it down Kendal Avenue forty years ago. Alan was going to stand up the back, and do his mushing, and I was going to sit in the body, on a little hanging seat a few inches above the ground, at dog-bollock level.

Right up close and grasping them now around their squirming bony ribcages, I could feel that these were mere slips of dogs, skinny, almost weightless, stick-boned whelps. But when the team were tied on, the only thing holding us back was a sort of ground anchor, literally roping us to the base camp. Nobody started them. It wasn't a question of 'Off we go', or 'Hup', or 'Mush' or 'Take it away, boys'. The engine was running. We were tied to the wall. It was clearly the wall or them. The noise was at airbus take-off level.

We would have to go soon, just to get the yelping under control. The ones who were going out were barking and pulling. The ones who were staying home were barking and running around, barking, to get a look and wagging their tails, and barking a bit more loudly just to make sure their bark could be heard above every other dog barking. The noise was so utterly overwhelming that after a few minutes I longed to get away from the place as much as any of the dogs did.

We lurched out of the trap at seventy miles an hour. I exaggerate. Sixty-nine miles an hour perhaps. I assume the smothering snow usually smoothes and blanks the whole slithering motion but with no snow here, no track to make note of either, just a sort of hard, dried, ploughed bit of field, we hit the first hump flying and banged over the next hundred in under half a second.

We did two laps of the circuit and I never once relinquished my iron grip on the grab rails by my seat. There seemed to be two speeds: fast and faster. Unlike my dog, these boys never stopped to smell a bush or pee on the side of a tree. Alan suddenly braked and stopped us for a moment or two. He took one of the dogs out. It was over-excited and over-heating. It was like removing a cylinder from an engine. We mushed and charged on. I was relieved that we didn't see a cat or a squirrel. We would have become airborne. What do I mean? I was airborne for a good proportion of the circuit, taking off over roots and skidding on one wheel round corners through the woods.

Finally we rumbled back to the compound. The dogs returned to their kennels for some refreshing Eukanuba and I went back to the hotel to rest my pulverized arse. I knew that there was still snow somewhere. But it was way up the mountain. We would have to go up to find it.

The night porter watched while I waited for my key. He came over and leaned in, in a conspiratorial fashion. Was I the one who wrote for the *Sunday Telegraph*?

'Yes. Yes, that is me, as a matter of fact,' I replied.

'I thought so,' he said, and paused. 'I don't like humour.'

I nodded. 'Right. I'll try to be less funny,' I said, and pointed to the keys behind the desk. 'I'm 124.'

'You don't look a day over forty,' the receptionist replied.

The porter turned away – a slight tremor of disgust curling the edges of his mouth.

We were late in the season, but the central heating was still pumping it out. After I had wrestled the quilt off my bed to prevent myself turning into a Pop Tart, and eventually worked out how to switch off the lights, I discovered that there was no way of pulling the curtains quite shut. So it was the dawn light that woke me. I had a shower, grappling with two unmarked handles and a range between ice-cold and 'Is that the emergency burns unit?'

It was midweek. After kippers and porridge, the funicular railway took me and a variety of elderly unemployed gentlemen up to the slopes while a cheery guide explained the advantages of the system in a mildly intrusive manner.

May Day was still a few weeks away. Posters brazenly advertised what was apparently still to come – a vision of white-capped hills, snowploughs and kiddies frolicking on the piste. It seemed unduly optimistic to be expecting blizzards in the next few days, but Aviemore remains optimistic. The dog sledding was one attempt to look to an après-ski future. Andy Bateman, a tour guide and explorer, was taking me off to sample another. It was called 'snow touring'.

I was getting a little sceptical about a real 'arctic experience', but Andy showed that a little perseverance has its rewards. The Cairngorms are a vast plateau that covers an area the size of Central London. It took just a few hundred yards of easy

ABOVE: Outside the El Alamein shelter.
BELOW: Deep enough for a snow hole.

skiing to find ourselves leaving the playground of the resort behind us, dropping the café sitting forlornly in the thaw over the brow of the hill, and traversing away across white slopes into untamed Scotland.

We were carrying little rolls of stretchy skin material for attaching to the bottom of the skis. They were like fur, with the hair lying one way. Going down, you slid. Going up, all the little hairs worked to stop you dropping backwards. They were ghastly to fit on, with elasticated straps that had to be yanked over the horn of the ski, like giant sock suspenders on a plank. After a few unfortunate catapults we started sliding up the side of the hill.

Here was plenty of snow. Here were mountains. Here was a vista stretching away to a horizon of complete and satisfying bleakness. Within half an hour we were stepping up across a wide brow to a white cornice of a summit and I was

ABOVE: Like looking for frozen peas in an overworked chest freezer.

getting used to the severely decreased mobility of downhill racing with a couple of pieces of carpet attached to your skis. We slithered up to a stony crest and the El Alamein Hut, built by the 51st Highland Division. I rested and poured a coffee. The shelter was little more than a stone shed supported on rusting girders. There used to be a dozen similar ones scattered out here across the wastes, but the others had all been demolished. They had engendered a false sense of security. Tragically, a party of schoolgirls, instead of coming down off the mountain, had set out to try to reach one. All had perished of hypothermia in the night.

The freezing cold of the arctic waste was hardly mitigated by a few stones anyway, and we were in a valley of cold, cold stones. Scree cascaded down the slope below us. The other side of the deep cut was similarly grey and white, like a bleached old photograph, drained of colour, unremittingly unforgiving. It curved away for several miles off and around the side of the mountain. Beyond the escarpment the plateau rolled across a succession of black crests and frozen slopes. This was God's building site. There was nothing here but rubble and collapse. And we had the whole of the valley to ourselves.

Now we waddled up the virgin snow on the face of the Cairn Gorm mountain to the cornice at the top. To one side, the snow, now supposedly so rare, had built up a massive, overhanging ledge. We used the skins on the base of our skis to defy gravity, taking care not to stray accidentally on to the crest, where we might unwittingly embrace gravity again, by falling straight into the valley. It was April. We were no more than a few hours' journey from our start but felt isolated already. A track of tiny spattered footprints crossed in front of us.

'That's a ptarmigan,' Andy told me. 'You can see how the little feathers in the feet whisk away the snow at the back.'

I could. So I wasn't the first to waddle that way, after all.

Under the tor, at the top, where the rime stood out like horizontal molten candle wax, we took off our seal-skin under-skis and shussed down into the next narrow valley. Andy stopped. I fell over.

He was surveying the opposite bank. 'That looks perfect,' he said.

It did look perfect – 100 feet of pure banked snow. Andy handed me a natty yellow shovel. I clicked its ball catch into a lightweight aluminium handle and we marched off to dig a snow hole.

Andy produced a huge, elasticized magician's wand. He flicked it open into a rod about twelve feet long and started poking it around. 'There's about ten metres here,' he said.

So Andy started digging a big hole straight into the side of the drift and instructed me to do the same, fifteen feet along from him. It was like looking for frozen peas in an overworked chest freezer. After an hour we stopped, turned and shovelled sideways, until we met in the middle.

Solid packed snow, as most little boys and a few Inuit will tell you, is a hugely satisfying building material. A bit of slicing and chopping and a sizeable room began to appear. We could make shelves or cupboards. Obviously we were limited in our choice of colours, but a blue-tinged white was perfectly acceptable. It reflected the light from our candles. Once we had made ourselves a bear-sized hideaway we shut up my door with some blocks cut out from the floor, polished them up a bit to let in some light (our 'window') and Andy made a sort of entrance-way step down. It was a low area – utterly scientific, because cold air is heavy. So if you have a low area then most of the really cold air sinks into that, leaving the comparatively warm air lingering around your sleeping bag.

We didn't have a fire. The candles made it drip a bit. Our low area funnelled the cold away. I had stayed in bleaker hotel rooms with colder night porters. This was our very own ice-hotel. Part of my warming joy was the miracle of the experience. It worked. It was just.

Outside a gibbous moon hung in a clear sky. Inside I considered the fact that we were literally holed up. Indeed we were camped in a valley winningly called 'Margaret's Coffin'. This was in honour of a local lassie who fell in love with a hairy fellow from another clan. When her impertinent paramour was cut to pieces she threw herself to her doom somewhere hereabouts. But it was far too cold for ghosts to be wandering abroad without a therma-fleece. We were thoroughly snug, and I had my own tryst awaiting me on the morrow.

At about six o'clock the following evening I stood by the side of a lake, like a lovelorn lady in a Victorian novel. I was mooching about in the gathering dusk waiting for Henry. Henry was dilatory. He usually came around this time, but not always. He could not be relied upon. But still I stayed and paced the

ABOVE: A cup of coffee at the entrance to the show flat.
BELOW: Waiting for the cold air to fall into the special hole (and another cup of coffee).

water's edge. Just a glimpse, that's all I wanted.

Henry was a male osprey, one of a very few left, where once there had been many. The truth is that the Victorians had a cavalier attitude to fish-eating birds. It could charitably be seen as ignorance. They didn't realize that if they paid the locals to kill eagles and hunt down ospreys and kites in order to protect their game, then eventually the birds would disappear. It is a relatively recent idea that nature is a balanced system. It is a relatively recent idea that the wild is not an inexhaustible resource.

Now I stood gazing out into the white sky, jumping to attention whenever some lonely rook or seagull flapped past the pylons over the way until I ran out of fervour and decided that Henry was going to stand me up. And then, naturally, there he was – the distinctive feathery wing tips, the loping approach, the seagull dive-bombing him. This last bit was unexpected, but it certainly helped to identify Henry. Luckily I had Alph McGregor, the countryside ranger, with me (how do you think I knew about the feathery wings?). Alph explained that they were trying to make him drop the fish.

'But he hasn't got a fish.'

'Aye. They're not very bright.'

'Will he find a fish?'

'He should do. This is a fish farm.'

Henry did not take fish by the pound. He took fish by the ton. And he obligingly showed me how. Talons down, a quick swoop and Henry was off, carting supper back to his family.

His nest is a mile or so away, near a village called Boat of Garten. Henry had been and gone by the time we walked up a little woodland path past the architect-designed, and thus completely intrusive, visitor centre to the much more appealing wooden forward-observation post, like an ersatz border spy command in the old Eastern Europe, equipped with televisions, huge binoculars and blankets and bunks for the volunteer watchers. Somebody had been making heads out of Blu-tak. They were there day and night.

As we arrived Henry returned again with another trout. Yvonne Malcolm, a geography graduate working as a warden at the hide, told me it was the seventh that day. They ate the head and the brains and threw most of the rest out. Fussy

ABOVE: Henry takes another fish supper back to the missus and kids.
BELOW: Waiting in the dusk like a lovelorn lady in a Victorian novel.

kids, eh? And, having provided the delicacy of the evening ('Not trout again!'), Henry was banished to the next tree along.

I could clearly see his funny round head and hooked beak and the frill of ruffled feathers as he swayed about in family banishment like a drunk lady at Ascot. And unlike you, watching it on television, I didn't only get the best bits, I got the whole lot, the sense of time, order and sequence that made it real. It must be what everybody comes for. This was the real spectacle of the wild. Forty thousand a year come to be voyeurs.

I had one last appointment, and it was with Ben Nevis again. Twice I had failed to make it to the peak of what I had labelled a cosy icon of British mountainhood. Now I was going to do it the uncompromising way.

A climber, Mark Diggins, was waiting for me by the hut on the north side. The

frozen-waterfall effect had finished. The snow had gone. We were planning a straightforward grapple with the rocks, somewhere between the hill walking I had done in the far north and proper rock climbing. We would behave like monkeys, hands and feet in action at all times, maintaining balance, letting the legs do most of the work, reaching up for holds and ledges and ensuring that I never overstretched myself or failed to have at least three points of control at any one time – 'clambering', in fact.

Mark, who comes from Manchester, is an extremely experienced guide. He told me that he had started climbing as a boy, taken by his school. Now he finds it a little miracle that he is allowed to make a living by practising his sport full-time, but that belies his application and hard work. He has acquired a box of certificates. As an international mountain guide and avalanche expert he is allowed to take parties up the Matterhorn and the Eiger and into the Apennines, all of which he had done many times.

According to Mark, this north face compared favourably with the Matterhorn. Though it was not as high, the skills required were very much the same. This was all very gratifying. As long as I actually managed it I could tell people I had done something which was not so very different from the Matterhorn, even if it wasn't.

Everything was perfectly familiar, except that whereas the first time we had headed into the bowl of the mountain, now we swung away to the west, traversing along the cliff and gradually ascending a jumble of stony ledges and haphazard outcrops to a long, dropping ridge. It was misty and intermittently wet.

Mark stopped on the last bit of grass, a lonely island where a couple of sheep stood to one side willing us to go away, and we put on our helmets and 'roped up'. I had my ice axe in my left hand, like a truncated walking stick for jabbing at the upper slope, and a loop of rope in my other hand, to give a little flexibility. It was another peculiarity to add to the process. The ice axe never made me feel more secure; neither did the rope. They just made me clumsy and cack-handed. 'You want to walk the tightrope, sure. Now, carry this lump of foreshortened, jagged metal and unravel this coil as you do so, will you?'

The slope was pure, loose stone, the consistency of rough ash from a fire and about the same colour, slithery and crumbling. It was more fun when we got to the bouldery upper edge and started 'scrambling' upwards, because this was

LEFT: I finally get to climb the north face of Ben Nevis.

recognizably climbing. Instead of feeling uncomfortably precarious as we walked up an unsafe path, we were making dozens of minute decisions, looking out for holds, wedging toes, feeling for a good, strong hold, clambering around the outside of a slippery rock and progressing ever on and up, up, up, over countless stones, piled one on top of the other, on a never-ending mad staircase.

There was a halt when we reached a slab-like ledge and Mark moved cautiously forward over the humped back of a significant protrusion. The clamber upwards had been so engrossing I had hardly bothered to look down or around, except to note that wraiths of smoke-like cloud would sometimes drift up alongside and between us and the immediate cliff faces to our left. But now Mark cautioned me to creep carefully after him and nodded downwards.

'It's about 1000 or so feet drop on that side,' he explained. 'I'm just going to make the rope fast here…' He began lashing us to a gnarled bump beside him. 'We have to lower ourselves down to the shelf there and get across to that wall over there.'

He tied off the knot and motioned me to follow, which was when I got the first real understanding of how far up we had come, sliding forward on my belly and

ABOVE: By the beginning of May the snow on the Cairngorm plateau is clearing.

peering over the brow at the stomach-tightening drop that fell away below us.

I felt no vertigo. The floor was dim and half out of focus because of the mist anyway. Perhaps I was beginning to feel happier with my rope, although there is an umbilical caution about the connection. Roped to another, you feel their precariousness too. If you go, so do they. It adds more responsibility than security.

But now I was going over the side, only a few feet down, but enough to make me scrabble with my feet and feel the quivering in my abdomen. The rope was tied round a fat belaying pinnacle. I could put all my weight on it. Mark followed. We crossed to the next gable of the roof of Scotland and then on and up, walking for a bit over some loose boulders, then across another sloping wall of boulders and on to a cloud-obscured top.

'This is what most mountain climbs are about,' Mark told me. 'Of course there are more and more difficult routes but you shouldn't think that getting up the biggest mountains is much more than this sort of terrain for most of the way. You've done a proper bit of climbing.'

And we were facing a cairn on a level stone field. I proudly reached down and lifted a stone and placed it on top. Later someone watched the film and tutted, because cairns are becoming another form of intrusion, breaking into the perfect natural innocence of the high places. Thousands of others had done this trip before. Thousands would come after me. What if they all moved the stones around? I could quite see the point. But I confess at that moment, with the screens of mist closing in my horizons and nothing around me but the bare lichen-spattered rock and the memory of the past three hours, I felt that Mark and I might have been the only people in the entire universe. I had gone as high as I could in the country of Great Britain, and it felt excellent.

THE LAKE DISTRICT

CHAPTER THREE

The Lake District

Now this is a wind. We're not high. We are close to the Duddon estuary, having crawled up through narrow lanes into a bare valley of the Lake District, a little distance from the warm securities of Windermere and Coniston, in the heart of the rougher hills that inspired Coleridge and daunted Wordsworth. It's cold and it's like being punched by an invisible thug every few seconds. Camera battery packs topple over. A bean bag sails across the field. Only the ever-present sheep seem unruffled.

Fifty-five stones – though there were, somebody has guessed, originally sixty – sit in a rough circle in a field. One weighs over five tons. Each is individually bedded in gravel – or was when they were first set up here some 5000 years ago. I am at Swinside stone circle. Brooding? Undoubtedly. Powerful? I think so. Mystifying? Well, it puzzles me. But it would be nice if it retained a little more of its mystery. Somehow, the enclosures of the eighteenth century, lovely though they are – the wall, the farm and the neat field – take away a little of the wild spookiness of the place.

I start walking around. The circle is not actually huge. It is about thirty paces across. But if I step back a few hundred yards (mind the sheep shit) I can easily gather some sense of its location. All the stone circles I have seen, in Wales, or the Lakes, or up in the islands, or in Brittany, seem placed with exemplary care – on high peninsulas or pinnacles, in slight valleys, or overlooking bays. Swinside, similarly, feels like a 'setting'.

The entrance to the circle is obvious. There are two extra stones marking it, and this we assume must have been the 'way in'. There might have been an avenue

RIGHT: What makes the landscape of the Lakes a source of inspiration?

leading up to it, it is said, of trees, naturally, but that has gone. The big, pointy stone which marks north is opposite the squarer, dumpy stone (the womanly stone as opposed to the phallic stone) which faces south. But, after that, all is conjecture. Whether the circle is connected on a ley line, whether it aligns with the Old Man of Coniston, whether a certain winter sunrise was meant to burst up through the entrance, whether it is a calendar or an abacus, all is speculation.

The people who built the stone circle didn't write. The stones themselves are their only record. The rocks sit there in the field, slightly sullenly, and offer nothing but themselves and, of course, their arrangement. So, naturally, when we start to ask questions we have to start with that arrangement.

Professional historians and archaeologists are not keen on magic and mystery. They prefer to rely on historical or scientific facts – like the fact that there was a discernible global warming around 5000 BC. This enabled Bronze Age man to exist up on the hills, so some historians engage in their own scientific prognostication. Perhaps, they say, the Bronze Age people built these things high up here, in this natural bowl, simply because it was sunny and they were living up here. Big stones were lying about. Why not make them into a circle, for a market, perhaps, or something totally mundane like a big house? Except, except… This goes against the evidence of the obvious trouble they went to.

It's called the theory of 'least effort'. These stones were not, in fact, just lying about. They were hauled here on log wheels with ropes made of leaves. Bronze Age man went to a lot of trouble to build these things. It now seems that the mammoth blocks that make up Stonehenge were dragged to Salisbury Plain from the Preseli hills in South Wales. That is a big effort for something which just looked pretty. Here in Swinside, they chose this site, this place. And on this freezing cold day it has majesty and awe on its side.

The stones told me, at the very least, that man has always sought spirituality in the mountains. Some historians of ideas imply that mountains and wild places were frightening until we were educated to think otherwise by poets and philosophers. But surely the poets and philosophers were only trying to articulate a feeling that we all experience? 'I will lift up mine eyes to the hills from whence cometh the Lord.'

The Lake District is probably the most inspiring patch of mountain territory in the world. Thousands of poems, hundreds of thousands of paintings and millions

LEFT: Trying to look manly next to the womanly stone – Swinside.

of words of guidance have poured out of the hills. Fourteen million visitors a year come to revel in their reputation. It was one of Britain's first National Parks. The National Trust owns 140 of its 885 square miles. (And that is all the Lake District is in extent, by the way, a mere back garden compared with the wastes of the Highlands). But, like a well-tended plot, it has infinite variety and delight. All agree that it is gorgeous. From the very beginnings of tourism, travellers came to marvel at it. Why?

Today some of that tourism has become quaint and antique in itself, like the steamboats that ply the lakes, with their glistening mahogany bright work, bimini tops, dorades and high funnels. The geologist Peter Nienow and I sat on the poop deck of the Raven under a flapping ensign on a cold, blustery, grey afternoon and watched the lovely shore of Ullswater slide by.

'It was like a giant upturned bowl,' Peter explained, using his blue fingers to shape an imaginary huge hump from some hundreds of millions of years ago. 'And the shape of it determined the drainage pattern.'

William Wordsworth was the first to note that the Lake District was arranged like a giant cartwheel with a central hub rising up to 3000 feet in the middle around Scafell, and the valleys radiating away like spokes.

'So why the Lakes?'

'Well, the valleys were cut by the glaciers and, because of the relatively shallow incline, instead of falling downwards they flowed out and scooped out the bottom of their tracks as they went.'

Dragging stones and boulders along with them, the glaciers scoured spoon-shaped depressions instead of steep clefts. These filled with water and created the lakes of the Lake District.

For me this wasn't quite enough explanation. There were lochs and very beautiful ones in Scotland. There were rivers and trees there too. But here the farms have settled into the dips and snuggled into the corners in a satisfying organic way, adapting their field shapes to the contours of the valley. They have released their sheep on to the high pastures and this has given them a cropped and shapely outline. It is this continuing contrast between the bare uplands and the cosy, embracing, comforting, green, prosperous, human-sized, planned and controlled lowlands which seems to excite people.

Peter and I went below to the smelly bar in the overheated cabin. He told me he had first come to the place as a child and still got a thrill coming back. It was indeed wonderful to see the side of a mountain slither by outside the porthole and catch a glimpse of a few yellow birch trees sneaking along the shore, but it was also exciting to see a little wooden jetty and boat, or a house surrounded by a block of trees and a path snaking up over a crest. This landscape had inspired him to become a geologist, to find out what had created it. 'It was great explorer country,' he said.

Yes, I think that nailed it for me. The great appeal of the Lakes was, in fact, over there, where the side of that hill disappeared into a wooded top. It was following the ridge to the top of the plateau into a miniature, fantasy world of mountains, rivers, hidden valleys, deep woods, waterfalls and high passes. You had to enter into it, adventure and go. That's what the ice age had provided for all of us.

ABOVE: Cropped uplands, cosy lowlands and great reflecting mirrors. Fourteen million people a year come to the Lake District.

As for me, I had to go too. I was intending to advance my climbing skills. So far, on my journey, I had walked. I had trudged. I had even used my hands on a few occasions, but I had not yet really dangled and heaved and balanced on little ledges, while tied on with ropes. It was time to rectify this.

I met Phil Poole, my instructor, and we advanced on a range of limestone cliffs, well to the east of the Lakes, out towards Penrith. 'Are you scared of heights?' Phil asked.

'No,' I replied. 'I'm scared of falling off.'

'We're going to start with a bit of "bouldering",' he said.

'The hottest August on record', as promised by the newspapers, had turned into a continuous dank and freezing shower. But we were temporarily dry this morning, under a low, black sky. Trekking up, past a disused quarry, our path was bisected by

ABOVE: Wastwater, looking towards the head of the lake.

a white, limestone drystone wall. Up higher, we finally got to another wall, but this was a natural one – a vertical slab of crusted grey stone.

'What's that?' I said. We had sat down and I was changing into my new, dainty rock-climbing shoes with pointy toes and asymmetric sides and black chewing-gum soles. I pointed to what I thought, without my glasses, was a paper cup or a piece of litter on the wall.

Phil peered. 'That's a bit of broken rock,' he said. 'The stone weathers grey, but where it breaks it's pure white.'

This was because the rock was limestone – a crushed mass of fish bones. We were sitting at the bottom of a dead sea. But I had already learned that that was probably on another part of the planet and in a completely different time zone.

I went to the wall. It was no more than a bank, about ten feet high. Phil jumped up and joined me. 'You can either be a slug or a stick insect,' Phil explained over his shoulder as he clambered up to clutch on to its side like a spider.

He showed me how a slug clings, and a stick insect sticks its arse out, but a proper climber relaxes and looks at his feet. Bouldering, it seemed, was a process of progressing along or across low faces of rock, balancing on tiny outcrops or almost invisible blips, trusting in the grip of the magic shoes and getting the fingers around blobby, wind- and weather-worn bumps at head height, staying no higher than you can safely fall.

Close to, it was easy to see that there were plenty of holds available and I crabbed delicately and ponderously along, clambering out around an ash tree which had squeezed itself and its roots into the rock. There were some tricky blank slabs and overhanging clumps, but I thought it was easy. I could do this. I could clamber sideways. I could progress. I had some childish memory of the big larch at the end of the garden. No, no, apparently I was a natural. I felt secure. Then we went down to the proper cliff.

I had hardly noticed this cliff. I had thought the bank we were practising on was the real thing, but Phil led me down a steep incline, through some trees, and I realized why we had climbed so high originally. Here was another wall. It was about thirty feet tall and looked a little slippery in the misty drizzle. Phil fished about in his pack, produced some silly helmets for both of us and, like a fetishistic witch doctor, started decorating himself with climbing bling: little squarish lumps on coloured ribbon, gold hoops, red and shiny hooks and indented bracelets of flat, silvery white metal on wires. These were his nuts and belays. He would slide the metal squares into rocks, where they would wedge and provide purchase. Then he would attach shackles and feed ropes through them.

Phil secured himself to a rope and the rope to me, and then he tied me to a tree as an anchor and set off upwards, very vertically upwards. It wasn't that far. The tops of contorted ash trees only just poked above the cliff. But it was steep.

I paid out the purple braided rope, which passed through my own harness, while Phil grunted a little and heaved himself upwards through flobby rain pellets. Turning up, I could feel them whistling from unimagined heights straight on to my face. The dry spell had ended. The rain was back. I sat there feeling impatient to get on up, even though the only thing slowing Phil down was the necessity to push some of his jingling adornment of nuts into the cracks. This was so that if he fell (or more likely, I supposed, if I fell) it would only be a short way before the wedge of metal arrested things.

When he finally shouted to follow, I could barely see him through the rain. But what a change. Instead of traversing I was now working upwards. Instead of the crusty, dry, cake-like plaster of Paris, the rock seemed like a gooey, sludgy harbour wall. And I was heaving myself well above my own height. So I had to stretch and pull and yank upwards. And then, after getting past the first slab and balancing precariously on a slippery toenail of rock, it was my job to pull out the little square of metal from the crack where it had been lodged.

To get it free required some sort of purchase. I couldn't get my fingers in there. And anyway I needed my fingers, to hold on to the sticky wet toilet edge somewhere at full stretch above my head, because my right foot, stuck out on a leg at seven o'clock, wasn't really gripping on the eighth-of-an-inch 'foothold' that was supposed to support me.

I yanked it out but it left me exhausted. And now I had to do the difficult bit of the climb. Up and out and around a bit that hung outwards and sideways.

'Don't use your knees,' said Phil, and then, after I had, 'You mustn't really pull on the rope.'

But this small manoeuvre wasn't like reaching a secure ledge. It was like going from a scary, nearly falling-off place to a slightly more scary clinging-on place.

RIGHT: Looking forward to Great Gable and my climb up Nape's Needle.

'I'm just about all right if I hug the side of this flat rock with my fingers in that far crack but I can't move any single limb now or I will fall and my strength doesn't seem to be holding me,' I said in a modulated tone to Phil, who nodded sympathetically.

The side of my face was flat against the rock. My legs were trembling ('sewing machine legs', according to Phil) and my left foot, the one with all the weight on, was definitely beginning to slide off the little finger of rock. But, from this starfish position, I was supposed to go on, and reach up for another hold. Surely not? It was impossible. I was tied on. I was perfectly safe. But this was hardly the point. I really did not want to slip and bash myself against this horrible surface, any more than you would want to fall head first on to a pavement. But the other reason was to do with pride. I had to be able to do this thing.

So I heaved. I wrenched myself. I used my knees and the rope and my stomach and I broke fingernails and scraped knuckles and kneecaps until I could wriggle over the parapet.

I got to the top, a mere thirty feet, an undignified, sopping, dirty mess, and sat, bruised and aching, on the grass in the rain.

'How was that?' Phil asked. 'Feel good?'

'Not good.'

So this was a summit. Far from being elated, I felt disappointed with myself. We were going to climb Napes Needle soon, but quite honestly I was beginning to wonder whether I was up for this.

As it happened, we delayed going up the mountain because of the rain. Did I say the rain? Up here in the Lakes, 'rain' is not a separate entity. It is a haze. It is a condition. It is the prevailing state of wet and wetness. It is Cumbria on a soggy day.

So we went into town. Despite expectations, bad weather is good for Keswick. The holiday crowd don their all-weather, techno-sport outer shell (anoraks) and, only too aware of their off-putting day-glo appearance, join the perpetual search for a better one.

They have plenty of choice in Keswick. Every other shop sells outdoor equipment. The glistening pedestrianized centre is thronged with glistening pedestrians. They mooch in and out of Blacks or North Face or Rohan: a restless, soggy mob.

I went to buy some local sweets at Ye Olde Friars sweetie shop instead.

Kendal Mint Cake is potent stuff. A climber needs lots of energy, and sweets are a quick way of getting a necessary carbohydrate boost, while comprehensively rotting your teeth. The first casualty of climbing is your molars. It's a good excuse. Climb, munch, climb a bit more, munch a bit more. Mm. Sweeties! But mint cake tastes like petrified toothpaste. And here in front of me were giant bars, chocolate-covered bars, luxury bars, brown cake and white cake. Rather than eat the stuff, I went to make some instead.

You can't enter a confectionery factory without being made to dress like Will Young. I was handed a bright-white trilby with a mesh crown and introduced to Dave Goodyear, only Dave was in white fatigues and sported an altogether different hat. It was a sort of floppy white flat cap like the drunken baker's in *Viz*. 'Am I wearing a gaffer's hat, Dave?' I asked. He laughed.

RIGHT: Natural materials complement the Cumbrian mountains as nothing else can.

I liked Dave. He was cheery and practical and answered every fatuous question about mint cake with enthusiasm, even pride, though he was more a fudge man these days – making flavoured fudges and chocolate truffle logs somewhere else in the sheds round the back of Kendal – ('It's not just mint cake here at Quiggin's, you know'). Dave even ate the stuff. But not on the job. I examined his teeth. All his own, I could tell.

Quiggin's were by no means the original mint cake producers, but they had been making it since 1880. (There was a non-aggression pact with the other Kendal manufacturers.) Just after the last war they had introduced the rubber moulds ('a bit of a Godsend really'). Before that they just laid it out in one gigantic slab and cut it by hand with a knife. Otherwise nothing much had changed.

ABOVE: I practise unloading invisible bags of sugar into the magic pot.

They used natural ingredients. I can vouch for that. Sugar is natural. And Kendal Mint Cake is pretty much wholly rearranged cane sugar. Dave and the manager laughed at the idea of sugar beet, but only because they had tried it once. 'It came up all frothing.' They waved their hands to demonstrate the way the monster confection had expanded out of the bowl. The bowl itself was Dave's first priority. He knew that he wouldn't have to kill me, once he had given me the secret of the recipe, because anyone who tried to make it would undoubtedly use a stainless-steel bowl, whereas a copper bowl, this very copper bowl, the bowl employed since the 1920s, was the only possible crucible for making the mint cake and Quiggin's had it, while lesser manufacturers did not.

Into this invaluable tub went five litres of water and then a handful of glucose syrup. This substance looked unnatural to me, although it was made from corn starch and was, I dimly remembered, little more than sugar itself. It sat in a large bucket by our feet, utterly transparent and with the consistency of melted glass. Dave showed me how he got a hold of it and then invited me to do the same – a little bit of a test for me – since I had to wet my hands and grapple a massive globule of the stuff up to the surface.

'Keep those hands moving, that's the way,' Dave cooed and I was really rather gratified that I managed to get a puppy-sized lump of coagulated, see-through goo into the copper without dripping more than a dozen indelible splodges on to my trousers and shoes.

If the process was originally discovered by accident, Dave left nothing to chance nowadays. He carefully weighed out fifteen kilos of pure cane sugar and watched as the temperature rose steadily to 127 degrees. In fact we all watched. I became quite tense. It took about five minutes. By now the sugar had melted. The mixture was clear, if seething. It was lifted from the gas and set to one side and little balls of fondant, standing by on a tray, were plopped in.

'So what does that do?'

Dave turned and with huge satisfaction said, 'Just wait and see.'

I was handed a wooden spoon and watched carefully as the fondant turned the mixture a vile off-yellow hue.

'Stir it up,' Dave urged and I did. 'That's it.'

And now we added the peppermint. Made to a secret recipe, it whopped up the nose with a punch like Bruce Lee. Tears started to my eyes. A strong pain crossed the internal bridges of my nose. I reeled from foot to foot.

But it was done. I blew my nose. The faint white snowman figure of Dave appeared through the potent mist. He took a big jug, scooped up the mixture, and trotted away to the metal-topped slab tables where row after row of rubber moulds sat edge to edge. He started slopping his hot sludge into the squared-off hollows. I was surprised there was so little portion control. One side of the mould was open to the air and Dave poured until the mixture rose in a little meniscus over the lip. Five minutes later the slabs were hard enough to be plinked out and laid in rows in a tray. Mmm! Solidified, zingy sucrose in a bar.

The following day, the climb was on. I was going up Napes Needle. This was a shard of rock sticking up out of the side of Great Gable, a mountain that overlooks Wasdale, and I was to have my photograph taken by Gordon Stainforth while doing it.

Now Wasdale is breathtaking. Driving around there for the first time, I thought we must have gone the wrong way. Where were the lakes? What had happened to the mountains? We were leaving the cosy certainties of Windermere, Dove Cottage and Ye Olde Lakeside Tea Shoppe altogether. In fact we were skirting the western range and heading right out towards Cockermouth, across much flatter, uninteresting country, so that we could come up into the valley from the West. It's a one-way street into Wasdale. Wastwater is a long, slinky loch, hemmed in by mountains on three sides, but as you come up from the coast it bursts out with an unexpected grandeur, the ridge to the south shoots straight down into the water and soon you are driving into a funnel. The end is stopped by a curtain of real mountains: Scafell and Great Gable and Kirk Fell. There is no road through them. They are the barrier that isolates Wasdale: a perfect scooped-out, enormous valley, with a lake in its floor, and a few farm buildings, a chapel and a hotel scattered across its expanse.

We were staying at that hotel, the Wasdale Head Inn, and in the hall the following morning I sat and tied on my boots beneath old photos in oak frames. They were mostly by two photographers called the Abraham brothers, and included, on closer inspection, one of the very entrance place where I now sat, taken some 100 years

RIGHT: The sides of Wastwater rise like massive walls.

ago. Next to that was one of Napes Needle itself. Two ladies in flowery hats stood on the top. Men in pipes lounged about the steep sides. The Abraham brothers had been the original climbing photographers. The hotel had been their base.

The boots in the photos were the essence of climbing in the Abrahams' times. There are plenty of people who might prefer a hobnail boot to go fell walking even today, but few serious climbers would trust themselves to tricorn nails. Even fewer would go scrambling up gullies or heaving themselves up rocks in a tweed suit complete with waistcoat, tie and a pork pie hat, like prep-school masters in a vertical assembly.

For me, it was back into my ankle-hugging, modern, moulded climbing footwear – shaped like a suede-covered car and soled with a black rubber substance with the resilience of a cricket ball.

Feet are crucial on a mountain climb. Feet and thighs. By now I was used to the routine. The steady rise through the fields, swiftly leaving trees behind, hedges behind, fences and horizontal detail behind, giving way to a sort of blankness, as the last field gate closes behind you. It's a long way. The slope rises.

On Great Gable we stuttered upwards for several hundred feet, through an empty landscape of sloping planes and rough sedge grass, with an occasional rock outcrop. If you can drag your eyes away from the obstacle course of jagged stones at your feet you can contemplate the increasing absurdity of the mass you are trudging up.

No photograph can really bring you close to the sheer volume. On the lower slopes you are in the in-between regions and rise quickly. The houses become models. The lakes become lower floors. The trees little balls of inconsequence. And because of the lack of significant detail, like stones or fences, the big, swelling tummy of the mountain is finally all.

In spring the perfect green miniature bushes of bilberry leaves, half the height of my boots, quiver with fluttering intensity. Little reddish ferns jiggle in the wind. In September the clumps of grass are spiked by long-stalked mini-mushrooms – mycenae mostly, hallucinogenic probably. They grow on sheep droppings but are far too sensible to burst into great, flat meadow horse-mushroom sizes. They remain tiny, evil-looking elf caps. You can see why this was seen to be the abode of little people. On this monstrous extrusion, the living world shrinks to a detailed carpet.

It is unexpectedly wet as well. For all their evident pitch, mountains drain abysmally. If you venture off the path, you're likely to be trudging through a sloppy bog. Every hollow holds a peaty marsh. The folds in the surface of the matted tussocks ooze and exude water as if the entire massive frame is wrapped up in a flannel sponge. There are sheep everywhere, dotting the areas where we will never tread. Spread out across the lower slopes, they are dutiful lawnmowers keeping the whole sodden blanket under control.

But all that happens for us at this stage is a steady trudge upwards. Edward Whymper, an early climber in the Alps, described climbing as 'largely toil'. For Sir Leslie Stephen, one of the founder members of the Alpine Club, it was this hard labour that separated the high-minded from the bottom-dweller. Only the moral and virtuous would ever go to the effort of making the struggle. As well as being actually separate, climbers, he felt, were psychologically separate too. They went up in order to look down on the rest of the human race.

Gordon and I chatted as we stepped upwards. He had graduated to photography after climbing with his brother as a teenager. He may have been using modern digital cameras to record the mountains, but their spiritual and inspirational qualities were still vital to him.

'You have to read Burke,' he told me. 'Burke introduced the idea of "the sublime".' We stopped for breath. 'All the eighteenth-century intellectuals that came after him liked to contemplate the "horrid" precipices. They stood in great storms because the excitement brought them closer to their own mortality.'

They were there for the thrill. Words like 'horrid' and 'awe-inspiring' were invented to try to explain the feelings. For the first time, in the mid-eighteenth century, intellectuals like the poet Thomas Gray took long and elaborate journeys into high places simply in order to confront the power of Nature. It was an opportunity to experience the great forces of God in the Universe and thus be humbled by the Universe itself. It was like bungee jumping to get closer to the meaning of life,

Gordon's photographs often showed seemingly empty cliffs with a tiny scrap of orange or red on them, which proved, on inspection, to be a human being, a climber, impossibly small on such a vast face.

We stopped at the end of the first track to swing back on ourselves in a big zig to our previous zag. There was time to turn and look back down the valley and wonder at how far we had risen by such steady unshowy grind. We could look across at the wall of hill on the other side, and marvel at the great falls of scree that seemed to bleed the mountainside and turn the process of erosion into a giant pattern.

But then, after 1000 feet, we were suddenly at an event. The blankness went. What looked from a distance a conical smooth top was far from anything of the sort. Suddenly we came upon a massive boulder, then another, as if we were approaching the site of a geological accident – as we were. The evidence became overwhelming. The top of the mountain had been assaulted by various forms of weather. Sometimes these were ice ages from thousands of years ago, sometimes winter snows from quite recently. The ice and the water had been cracking and splitting the tops for ever.

'What I like about the top of a mountain is this individuality.' Gordon had his camera out now and was photographing God's sculptures. 'Each summit is completely different. But if you look from below you would never realize how complicated it was up here.'

On Great Gable the central hole we were heading for was a wet and muddy series of loose stones, and we were clambering up towards it; using our hands to steady ourselves, putting arms above us to grasp at outcrops in the red mud, watching our feet to ensure that the spit of wet rock we were about to put a foot on was not going to dislodge from the wall.

Looking down, I realized that we were very high up. And this last cliff was finally what I had come to surmount.

Napes Needle emerges from a typical broken area, but it goes on up to a phallic pinnacle. Now, instead of trudging and clambering we were going to climb.

Gordon clambered on to a balcony, called 'the Dress Circle', on the far side of the mountain and Phil roped me up.

I would sit as the anchor, while Phil got up ahead. He would tie off various ropes and make sure that everything was secure and then I would follow.

This was simple enough. I sat, and watched as he grunted and heaved himself up the first section to a little ledge. There were holds and it was a little steep, so clearly I would have to 'go for it' and overcome any 'horridness' or 'terrible' feelings brought on by hanging out over 1000 feet of cliff. The holds were quite evenly spaced and seemed simple enough. I mean, I could at least see them. Above that sat another huge rock, apparently balanced on top of this plinth, and this, the needle itself, had a crack running up it.

Sitting down on the ledge below, all tied up and wearing my white helmet, I

watched as Phil stuck his foot into the crack, took hold of a protrusion above his head and with a few grunts marched up the crack and over the ledge. I felt distinctly like Stan Laurel. I had to assume an expression of patience while gormlessly holding on to the other end of the rope, waiting for Oliver to fall off and whisk me off the ground into a hilarious accident. But that didn't happen. After a while I heard Phil shout. He had tied the rope right round the top end of the needle and now it was my turn. So off I went.

Once again, despite being no more than six feet off my first ledge, the sense of being up and vulnerable began to alter everything. I could get my feet on the various holds. I could reach up and get hold of the slithery triangles of rock above me, though they were a little more slippery than I had expected, and I was much weaker than I thought, but with an exhausting heave and a suitably sublime

ABOVE: Time to marvel at a great fall of scree on the side of Great Gable.

wobble I managed to get up the first bit. Now here was the crack. This was a little dodgy. For starters the crack went off at an angle, so the idea seemed to be that you 'walked' up the bottom edge of it, as if it were a sloping, steep branch. And you kept your balance by... I looked up and felt about on the rock face. There was nothing there, or at least there were minuscule wrinkles. But I could hardly trust to my feet without a little more than a fingertip wedged on a wrinkle, could I?

There were encouraging shouts from Gordon on the other side of the ravine, which rather indicated that I could, or should.

Phil's voice joined in from out of sight, up above. 'Now just go up the crack.'

'Well, OK.' I tippy-toed along, feeling ghastly. I was just balanced on these smooth ridges, not really on them at all. But now the crack was getting vertical. It wasn't a huge crack. It was about six inches wide. At the bend, I had my left foot wedged on the turn, one hand stretched out to some hopeless pimple on my far right and the other gripping a peanut out to my left. I could understand the principle. Just like Phil I would stick my foot into the crack, get a purchase on the rock inside and then climb up it like a ladder.

Quite frankly, this was as precarious a situation as I ever wanted to be in. I was mighty glad to have reached the corner of the crack. I could get more grip once I had got my right leg on to something. So I tentatively stuck my foot inside

the dark space. There was nothing there.

I suppose it should have been obvious. It was a crack. The enormous rock I was climbing had been split apart, and like most splits, this split ran right the way through. But when I watched Phil do it I had imagined that he was putting his foot on some rocks wedged inside it, or a ledge, or something, or anything. I had my own foot in there now and like a fool looking for a light switch in the dark I moved it around and up and down the smooth sides of the crack, searching for a purchase, except that there didn't appear to be one.

'You have to wedge your foot in,' Phil called down invisibly from above.

'OK,' I called invisibly from below. My foot was invisible too. This was the blind leading the blind leading the blind. Wedge my foot in it? What on earth was the man talking about? But eventually, by twisting it on its side, I somehow got my poor foot uncomfortably stuck in a part of the crack. It was painful and hardly secure.

'Now move your other foot up. There's a hold on the side of the crack,' Gordon was shouting from across the mountain.

'OK.'

I was answering 'OK' to any instructions now, but in that slightly querulous tone that a voice adopts when a body doesn't believe that it can do something and the mind refuses to give way to complete panic. My fingers were hurting with holding on so much. But, yes, I could get my other foot on that tiny, spiky nodule, just about, as long as I crammed my legs into each other.

'Now move your right foot above that.'

'Er … OK.'

What he seemed to mean was that I had to lift my right leg up the crack, above my trembling left leg, and the ladder effect would start, but I couldn't do it. My thighs were too big. If I pulled my leg upwards, the upper, fat part of it simply stuck fast in the crack. This was no good. No, no.

'You have to move your hands up, get a hold of the hold up there, that's right … higher … there.'

It was another half peanut.

'And now use that to pull yourself up until you can get your leg out.'

There was a long pause. But I was muttering to myself now. I was saying things

LEFT: One fat leg stuck in an enormous crack. It's not as easy as it looks.

like, 'This is impossible. I just can't do this. It's beyond me. I'm not a climber. I'm fifty-two.' I hope they were loud enough to be recorded by the sound man, and later, when they scraped my mangled corpse off the valley bottom, they could be played at the inquest and shame the executive producers who had forced a one-time book-programme presenter and comic to his untimely death. Except, of course, I was roped on. Damn. So I wouldn't even have that satisfaction.

'OK,' I said aloud.

But in the meantime I tried to heave myself up sufficiently to free my podgy right leg from the crack. This was like school gym. I could not do the heave-ups then either. My left arm, never my strongest limb, was at full stretch above my head and I was expected to use it to heave the rest of my body up two or three feet. I was muttering again. 'I can't. I should never have tried. What am I doing?'

I hung there and considered my options for an awfully long time.

'OK?'

'OK.'

I wasn't OK at all. I was completely buggered. Phil pulled a bit on the rope. And then I heaved and scraped my way on. I felt like I was forcing my torso a little higher by sheer willpower, hugging the entire mountain now, until by some sort of inhuman effort, and probably a bit of illegal yanking from Phil too, I managed to get my elbow over the ledge and ignominiously heave the rest of me after it. Finally I was sitting on the ledge, worn to a frazzle and holding on to the topmost boulder as if it were a lifebelt in a sea accident.

Despite all my ropes and belays, and convinced I was going to fall off, I just about managed to stand on my jelly legs and pretend to look nonchalant for Gordon's camera. It was my lowest point. Instead of feeling elated at my conquest, I felt humiliated and slightly depressed, just as I had in the gym thirty-five years before.

Gordon, all the mountaineers and the camera crew on the other side applauded loudly.

That only made it distinctly worse.

'It's difficult,' Phil was saying by way of consolation. 'There aren't a lot of handholds. You have to use your knees and things to slither up.'

'I used everything,' I said. 'I used my cock.'

The following morning I felt in need of a little homely security and took comfort in a bus. At nine o'clock I waited at a stop by a bridge in the rain with Barry Surtees and Bush the dog, a Staffordshire bull terrier.

'There's nothing as restful as a slow bus. Especially a stopping one.' Alfred Wainwright had written. He always took the bus home after one of his walks, which had to finish by nine, so that he could guarantee a ride. And (parp, parp) a slow bus is an excellent way to travel – the feeling of community, even when empty, the dignified rumbling progress, the sense of being slightly, peripherally joined to other people's lives.

We were on a 'special' for the telly, so the only other two passengers on the bus were Ted and a man with glasses. They were both officials of the bus company. I didn't mind. It was a stately carriage. We held up the traffic and trundled on under dripping trees. The Lake District morphed beautifully from dark, sculptural

ABOVE: Pretending to look nonchalant nowhere near the top of Nape's Needle.

oak wood to delicate fields to high heather and bracken and grass, and then out on to a bleak upper level where a huddle of sheds and car parks in an appropriately utilitarian setting announced that we had arrived at the Honister Slate Mine.

I got off and walked into a shop. It displayed 1001 uses of slate: bottle holders, bottle coolers, carvings of fairies, house numbers, knives, cheeseboards, serving platters, whole fountains, worktops, poetry, key rings. One thousand and one uses of a four-million-year-old lump of compressed volcanic ash. I think, but I'm not sure, that I even spotted a roof tile in there somewhere. This was once, of course, the one and only use of slate.

Barry and Bush, the marketing arm of the enterprise, introduced me to Mark Weir, the owner. Mark had trained as a helicopter pilot. His grandfather had worked down the slate mine. Mark was flying over the site one day and said to himself, as you do, 'I could start that mine up again and run it myself.' So he bought it.

We walked over to his workshop by the public entrance to the mine. Mark threw me a lump of slate to grip between my knees, put a chisel in my hand and urged me to split it. I had to lay the edge of the chisel along a cut edge, tap it and ease the chisel into the crack. Obviously, if you are an expert, as Mark was and as his grandfather was before him, then you simply knocked once, and a neat piece broke off. The bit I was fiddling with was half an inch thick.

'Come on,' said Mark, 'you should be able to get five slates out of that. You push it in. Now tap again.'

My slab split with a satisfying kerplunk, but my slate was far from perfect. Somehow I had managed to end up with a relief map of Cumbria, and this was the best slate in the world. Or, certainly, as far as Mark was concerned it was. It was very green and very special and had once been specifically used for important jobs like the roof of the Houses of Parliament.

From the Range Rovers and the crowds and the helicopter and Mark's general air of efficient plausibility, I somehow imagined that he had been rich when he bought the place – that this was the sort of company acquired by a successful City trader or supermarket millionaire or helicopter air-freight magnate. But Honister is not a 'gentleman's hobby slate mine'. Mark had put his life into it.

He led us away and up the hill, pointing out the workings, where little burrows disappeared into the other side of the valley and huge trails of waste fell away down the slope. 'I own those ones too and all these on this side here as well, but I don't work those,' he explained. 'My main problem is making sure that people don't injure themselves by exploring them.'

We came to a wide track through a fall of waste clinging to the side of the mountain.

'This is my road. I had to build it myself with a digger and three times it's been washed away. They kept trying to stop me. They said it was too dangerous, but I need to be able to get people down this way so they can come into the big workings.'

ABOVE: One satisfying 'kerplunk' and a pile of rubbish – cracking slate in Honister.

We snaked around the side of the hill and came to the entrance to the mine – little more than a big hole in the rock face. I heard voices. I looked up. A train of people in helmets were walking along a sort of rock balcony 100 feet above me, and disappearing into the mountain.

'That's one of the guided tours,' Mark explained.

It is not something you associate with the Lake District, but the most beautiful mountains in Britain were once the cradle of our industrial processes. The water fell in rushing torrents of power. The minerals were near the surface. There was plenty of wood for fuel. Ironically it was all over for mountainous Cumbria, as soon as the proper Industrial Revolution got going. Entrepreneurs realized that the minerals existed in the lower areas too. Slate mining continued as a lone survivor into the twentieth century, but the costs of labour and competition from China and Spain gradually killed it off. Mark had stumbled into an industry that was not only dying but one that people wanted to see dead.

'I had terrible trouble with the Park authorities,' he explained. 'They didn't want any industry in the beautiful Lake District. But this used to be the livelihood of the local village. I wanted to make it as a sort of monument. The life expectation of people who worked in these mines was no more than fifty. I owed it to them.'

He owed it to the bank as well. He had invested everything he had in the mine. We donned helmets and lights and walked in. Mark had widened this tunnel and blasted it out himself. As an owner, he discovered, he didn't need any licence to use blasting powder, but he had no idea how to do it. He called up his uncle, who tried to remember which wire went where. After a small, unfortunate earthquake they were soon blowing huge slabs out of the mine. But it was a daunting task.

'I used to come down here at night and lock myself in, and I'd just go at it, all alone on the JCB, all through the night, digging out the tunnel and the slate. I thought I was going to go crazy.'

We turned the corner and flared a light and I realized we had walked into a gigantic chamber. This was where the huge streaks of spoil came from. It was the size of a theatre. Every bit of the wall was scraped and chopped to shape. Slate is made of volcanic ash and mud, hence its fine grain. It has been compressed together by the shifting of tectonic plates which squash huge seams like ribbons through the earth's crust. Miners have to dig out the rock that surrounds it, and

ABOVE: Mark Weir and the light of experience.
BELOW: Inside the chamber of slate.

then the slate itself, looking for perfect square-on sections to work. There was plenty of slate that existed in slightly curved or rounded forms, but that was no good for the roofing business, so that had to be thrown away. That is why slate mines are surrounded by heaps of discarded, no-good slate, broken into flakes and fragments, sometimes huge and often of a frankly beguiling shape. I kept stooping to pick up book-sized slivers, green or purple or moody grey, which had split into pleasing triangular cones, or flat, perfect doorstops. Then I'd see another, better one, and throw the pieces I had away, filling my pockets with my own slate key rings, kitchen tops or paperweights.

'What I'm going to do here,' Mark explained, 'is make this into a giant stadium.'

So it was a theatre, after all.

ABOVE: Honister Slate Mine as Mark sees it from his helicopter.

'I've already chopped some of the more dangerous stuff off the ceiling because the men who cleaned this place out were just looking for the good slate. And they left these terrible hanging death traps. It was dangerous just blowing them off.'

But in the glory days, when they did get good slate, they used to bundle it down the hill to the works. There, a skilled slate splitter would make what was known as a bargain. He would bid for the block, calculating how many slates he thought he could get out of it, and undertake to produce them for an agreed price. Of course, if he failed he operated at a loss. For the mine owner, it kept skills up to scratch. For the worker, it meant poverty and hard work.

Mark was a driven, hyperactive ball of energy, interspersing his stories with tales of night landings in his Gazelle helicopter when the instrument lights died, of his arrest for parking offences, of his encounters with ghosts in the darkness of the mine when he was working at night. Thanks to him, Honister now has a thriving shop, the tour is a big attraction, visitors can practise splitting slates and soon they'll be able to see presentations about the history of the mine in Mark's huge underground amphitheatre. Honister produces 10,000 tons of green gold a year. The National Park may be worried about the idea of industry in their purlieus, but Mark had a crazed enthusiasm for the mine, the people and their history. In his own way, I had to admit, he was as inspired by the mountains as any Lake poet.

We went back to the Wasdale Hotel for the night, with the tiled floor and the painted bath. Dinner was chicken with field mushrooms in a cream sauce. I liked the cheese. All of which was ripe. And we got to bed early. And I dreamed dreams of falling off mountains.

The following morning we were joined by the Wasdale Mountain Rescue Team: Julian Carradice, Richard Warren, Penny Kirby and the dog, and the dog's puppy, which was a rescue dog in training. We left the car park like a small army, trekking up through slightly damp woods under a grey sky.

When we finally made it up to Scafell, after a hefty trudge along a carefully laid path, and a scramble through a steep and rotten gully, the shale breaking in our hands and crumbling in chocolate flakes beneath our feet, the sheep were there before us. They surmount the most inaccessible ridge and stand there, looking on with their unblinking eyes, which, close to, resolve into fuzzy-edged lozenge pupils, and give them an air of disturbed preoccupation.

'They come down from the peak,' Julian explained, waving above us. 'Sheep eat downwards, so they make their way down the ledges until they come to the edge and quite often they go over that as well.'

'So if enough go over they'd provide a soft landing for anybody who followed them.'

'Well, at the bottom of some of the gullies there can be quite a carpet of dead sheep.'

The poet Coleridge came down like a sheep. He walked up Scafell in 1802 as part of an excursion in the Lakes while he was living in Keswick. He was alone. He carried a knapsack with a couple of books and a change of cravat and he took the conventional, the easy, way up. Though in my opinion the easy way up to the top of England's highest mountain is not that simple. But Coleridge had 'an addiction', as he put it. He was always a man of unbridled appetite – for learning and literature, for sensual experiences – and for terrifying himself. This expressed itself in his decision to descend by any route which took his fancy, completely randomly – not something that the Mountain Rescue Service could approve of at all.

Broad Stand is an accident blackspot. 'It's often boy and girlfriends together.' Julian continued. 'She doesn't want to go but they're looking for a quick way across to Scafell Pike and they set off with easy drops to begin with – but they don't stay easy.'

This exactly mirrored the experience of 'the original rock-climber' Coleridge. He lowered himself down one ridge – a drop of seven feet, did the same on the next and then found himself looking at a twelve-foot fall. He made this by lowering himself as far as his fingertips would allow, and crashing the last six feet on to a ledge, where he lay trembling 'as if in a trance'. Looking up, he saw storm clouds and decided that, thanks to those great eighteenth-century attributes of will and reason, he need fear no longer. There was no reason to be afraid. His intelligence would see him through. It did. Perhaps he was more intelligent than the average hapless victim. He got down.

I did too, but on the end of a rope. It was horribly slippery up on that shelf in these wet conditions and easy to see how anybody could lose their footing. But

RIGHT: A snow-covered view of Scafell Pike and Dow Crag from Great Moss.

having made it to join up with the Mountain Rescue, I was tied up and encouraged to step over the side.

I have abseiled before. And it is easy. You stick a rope through a cunningly designed metal loop so that if you raise the right arm it gently slides through, with the friction controlling the rate of descent. Lower the arm and it stops, and so do you. Raise it and you go faster. But you have to put your weight on it. You have to trust the system. You have to lean right backwards, out into space, with your feet up against the rock, and let the rope take the strain.

And on Broad Stand it all came back. I leaned backwards and let myself jump down.

As it happens it wasn't straightforward. This abseil had a corner in it. This was a new concept. The staircase had a landing and another flight. I got down to the next ledge and then had to swivel round ninety degrees and start down the next level. But I lost control on the slippery face and went crashing into the rock.

Disappointingly, it hadn't all come back to me.

At the bottom there was a slit between the two rocks that I had to push myself through. It was called Fat Man's Agony. I don't believe Coleridge himself could ever have come by that route. When he lay down for a rest on the rock shelf he lamented that he had become extremely flabby.

The effusions of Wordsworth and Coleridge and their disciple Southey all helped to make the Lake District stupendously popular as a place of resort, but they weren't the first to come here.

Celia Fiennes tends to attract the adjective 'redoubtable'. A titled and rich lady of Chelsea, she was curious about the country she lived in and set off on a series of journeys to the far reaches of Britain about 150 years before Coleridge. She certainly had no intention of climbing any mountains. Like most commentators of her time, she was more nervous of wild places than enchanted by them. She got to the edge of Cumbria and rather wanted to hurry through it.

I reproduced a little of her travel in a coach and horses. This was hardly fair to the woman, since she more commonly rode side saddle on the back of a nag. Celia would have been grateful for our smart German carriage with its huge half-moon springs and high-stepping black thoroughbreds. But there weren't the roads for that sort of conveyance in her day.

Fred Harrison, who took me, drove the beasts as a hobby and bred them successfully. He farmed a few thousand family acres near Penrith. Naturally enough, as we filmed we had to go back and forth so the camera could get a proper shot, and Fred put Billy and Ben round and back, forwards and into reverse, with a quick twist of his fingers. He let me have a go, and I understood the exhilaration of what has recently become a sport rather than a flamboyant way of getting to market. His pair of trotters were so well schooled they were as pliable as a car and rather more easy to get into gear than my Vauxhall. Celia, on the other hand, complained that the pony she rode got exhausted by the route and needed a constant renewal of its shoes.

As Norman Nicholson, a more recent poet of the Lakes, pointed out, what makes Celia's account of the scenery she passed through on her way to Kendal so fascinating is that she doesn't have the hand-me-down poetic traveller's vocabulary

LEFT: Abseiling is like riding a bicycle. Get it wrong and you fall off.

to describe it. Writing before poets had grappled with the 'horrendous', the 'awesome' and the 'beetling', and well before philosophers had decided that we should exult in the proportions or the 'sublimity' or the 'spirit-awakening' qualities of the 'craggy summits', Celia saw only water, rocks and stones. She wrote that the water came down from high above and joined with other water, bouncing off rocks to make lots of water. To her it was pretty and confusing.

She was rather more interested in the villages, in the way that people lived and their recipes for cheese or bread. Before the coming of the Enlightenment, the outburst of 'rational' explanation for the mysteries of nature, and the vogue for 'big questions' about the origins of human feelings and responses, Celia and her fellow early travellers seemed to exhibit a sturdy, straightforward practicality. Daniel Defoe found 'a kind of inhospitable horror'. Wilkinson, a Quaker, looked at Cumbria and talked of 'the pyramids of God', but, before more sophisticated tourists came, the mountains were sometimes given personalities and names, though they were still places of malignant spirits. Celia looked at the hills and worried that they were waste land, uncultivated, pretty useless and best avoided.

It seems incredible to us that the nervous, early tourist should only have experienced such horrors in the cosy, green-valleyed, tree-lined and buttery Lake District. Didn't they find the place lovely at all? What transformation in ideas had to happen to allow Ruskin to write, a century later, that 'the only true natural scenery is mountain scenery'?

These days some of the most expensive hotels in Britain grace the shores of Windermere.

'We have a regular clientele who come to escape and know we offer complete privacy and that little extra luxury,' the manageress of the Samling Hotel explained as I checked in that evening. Her clientele didn't really need to go walking in the hills when they could fly over them in their helicopters. Each bedroom was the size of a small flat, or, in one or two cases, quite a large flat. Each had a different theme. I was unable to pinpoint mine. The furniture was heavy, brown-hued and rustic, the walls were a roughened russet colour and my bedroom was raised on a balcony to allow Errol Flynn to swing in from the light fitting – it was Cumbrian *Pirates of the Caribbean* mountain escapism of quite a different variety to the freedom envisaged by the Lake Poets.

I wandered lonely in a cloud,

Of floating linen sheets and down

And all at once…

I saw absolutely no crowds at all.

There were plenty of crowds in Windermere and up in Grasmere the following day. I don't think many of them thought of the Lakes as being too 'horrid'. Quite a lot of the 'trippers' seemed content to visit the historic named sites, with their car parks and souvenir shops, without ever going up to seek the solace of the hills that inspired them. Perhaps they find such places a little bit too effortful and wild.

I hadn't been to Dove Cottage myself for fifteen years but I remembered walking down a track to get off a main road and a simple, almost suburban, lane. I remembered the little white house too, when I finally found it.

I joined a party from an 'English as a foreign language' school and shuffled inside. With fifteen in our group, we were soon crammed into a tiny room at the back, which had been lined with newspapers and varnished golden brown. There we peered at the bric-a-brac of genius – a few pink bowls, a pair of glasses,

LEFT: At least Billy and Ben are looking where they're going.

Wordsworth's passport with the description in French: 'oval face' 'long nose'. These, and other characteristics, were supposed to stand in lieu of a picture.

Our own picture of the inhabitants of the cottage, pieced together from a few encased objects, was just as vague.

I liked the quiet, austere beauty, the dark-oak tables and the rag rugs. I liked them more than Mr Wordsworth's second-best wig, or his half-chewed pen, or the rest of the stuff in the cases. But very few people, especially writers, ever kept themselves as tidy as a museum, and as we jostled around we gained some idea of what it must have been like when William, his wife, his sister, the maids, De Quincey, Coleridge, Lamb and other passers-by all stayed overnight (as many as fifteen living together at any one time) in this tiny cottage. No wonder William himself took to the hills and spent so much of his time walking. It was while out that he practised the rhythms of the poetry in his head, before hurrying back to get his sister, Dorothy, to write them down.

'I somethinged lonely as a cloud, a rumpty, tumpt timpty hills, walk, walk, walk, walk.'

Thomas De Quincey, who arrived as student-disciple and stayed to be a dogsbody, calculated that Wordsworth must have trudged 200,000 miles by the time he was eighty. They were mainly local miles. Wordsworth wasn't Coleridge – off to the high peaks in search of shock and awe. He walked the low paths and fossicked in search of natural glory. He chose not to see it as an arrangement of shapes and forms (this was the rage for making pictures out of views, called 'the picturesque'). Nor did he subscribe to Edmund Burke's notion of the horrific and terrible. His poetry articulated his emotions:

There was time when meadow grove and stream,
The earth and every common sight,
To me did seem
Apparelled in celestial light.
The glory and the freshness of a dream.

His beliefs, so commonplace today, once had the glory and freshness of a dream themselves. He thought that we, as human beings, were linked completely with nature. Rocks and stones and trees and human beings 'rolled round in earth's diurnal course'. By exulting in hills and woods, and those daffodils nodding in the

RIGHT: Inside Dove Cottage today.

breeze, we could come close to the great power that had created the universe.

In one way this is hugely egotistical. Our excited emotional response to woods and thunderstorms and the moon and the trees is the presence of God in us. On the other hand it is completely unselfish. Mankind should not try to separate himself from the universe in order to command or control it, but accept that he is bound to it through a great moral thread. So we are extremely special in the universe, and can experience the most special spiritual presence from it.

Well, this is sort of what we all believe now, in a new-agey way. We are all Wordsworthians. *Life on Earth* is a Wordsworthian television programme. Generations of children have been forced outside on a Sunday afternoon because of Wordsworth's belief that going for that walk in the country is essentially 'good for you'.

'Unspoilt countryside' is a very Wordsworthian notion. He craved solitude. Though the Wordsworths seem to have run an ongoing, unpaid bed-and-breakfast service for their friends, he opposed the railway coming to the Lakes and bringing more city people from Lancashire. This was odd, because he wrote a guidebook himself. One slightly gormless clergyman tourist is supposed to have enquired of Matthew Arnold whether Wordsworth had ever written anything else.

Others have cherished his memory, his vision and his countryside. Ruskin, the great art critic and mountain lover, moved to the area and bought a house sight unseen, so convinced was he it would be lovely. Ruskin's assistant founded the National Trust to preserve the landscape. Beatrix Potter bought farms. Arthur Ransome came here on holiday and championed the glories of open-air holidays for children.

The appearance of the Lake District today owes a lot to the enclosure movements of the seventeenth and early eighteenth centuries. It was not really very old and traditional when Wordsworth wrote about it, or at least not as old and traditional as it is now. Like many writers he was seeking to preserve a golden vision which was fresh and new to him when he was a young man.

The legacy of this was brought home to me on Black Hall Farm, not far from Hardknott Pass. Could any place be more evocative of the world that inspired Wordsworth? Here was a little knot of trees by a gushing stream. Beyond that a gate and a long track (definitely not a drive) leading down to a group of simple

buildings, glistening under the morning sun in a crook of the valley. It was just one of ninety-three farms owned by the National Trust.

This one was looked after by Tony Temple, the tenant. As I walked up I was mobbed by dogs. There were three or four Jack Russells, leaping about in a frenzy, a geriatric collie nosing her way around the farmyard and a chorus of sheepdogs barking from kennels round the back somewhere.

It was the sheep I had come to look at. They were Herdwicks. I was going to accompany Tony as he took them out on to the high pastures, where they live for most of the year. They come down after lambing and are kept in byres to be sorted,

ABOVE: Rock-hopping above Wastwater.

taken to market and counted in the strange numbering system that derives from ancient Norse: 'yan, tan, tethera'.

Now Tony called to his dogs Bess, Jed and Laddie and they set off for work. The sheep were penned in a long, walled field beneath the farm, running down by the river. With a couple of whistles and a hup or two, the dogs shot off on duty. Charging up to the barbed-wire fence and sailing over it in a soaring bound, they got ahead of the sheep on the far end and started running out and around the flock, bringing them down towards the gate. The sheep quite simply don't like the dogs. They shuffle about in a panic, taking whatever route will get them as far as possible from these tiny, lean streaks of black-and-white menace.

Tony was there to chide the dogs, warning them when they had missed a posse, or had failed to spot a gap which might allow the sheep to run back the way they had come. He needed minimal instructions to send them off to the right or left, in wide, flanking manoeuvres. He could make them stay and stand guard, or trot by on sentinel duty. It was a relationship that had to be built up over years. The dogs were the most valuable things he possessed.

As I watched his precious workers lead the sheep up the track and towards the main road, where we would ford the stream, open a gate and head out towards the mountain, I could see that each dog had a completely different character. The youngest, Laddie, was like an over-enthusiastic camp guard. He rushed at the sheep on the slightest provocation, as if he hated them and wanted them to step out of line, so he could threaten them.

Tony pointed ahead, to a far wall, way up the flank. That's where the gate was and where he wanted his flock to be. It seemed a hopeless ambition. The terrified sheep scattered all over the hill. A vast area studded with bog and patches of bracken, it rolled down into invisible dips, but the dogs were ahead of the game. All we did was trudge slowly in the right direction and they rushed about assembling the sheep for us. Or at least two of them did. Tony stopped to call out Jed. 'There he is. You see he's getting older now. So he's getting lazy. I have to keep an eye on him because he's quite happy to find a bit of bracken and get down out of sight and let the others do the work for him.' But Jed had been spotted and now was put to work, for another pernickety assembly, by another gate in a long drystone wall.

RIGHT: A sheep's-eye view.

This wasn't a corner gate. It was right in the middle. The sheep all had to be kept to one end, so that when the gate opened they could walk through. Tess kept up position to stop them heading north, the others gathered in the strays and, when everybody was ready, they all lay down obediently at a carefully judged distance from the flock, covering all the possible exits, with their tongues lolling. Tony stepped forward and opened the gate. I felt he could have done it entirely in his own time. The dogs, having taken ten minutes to collect the sheep, seemed entirely capable of holding them together in that group for as long as was required.

This was as far as we were going. The sheep were released now and hurried away.

'They'll stay up and around this mountain here, they won't go far,' Tony explained. Herdwicks, as well as being hardy, are homing sheep. They are bred to be attached to a particular area. If they are taken off, they will make their way back to the bit of hill where they were born and raised. It is this unique instinct that makes farming with sheep like this possible at all, because the open grazing is just that, unfenced land that spreads for ten of thousands of acres.

I was surprised to find that Tony was not quite as attached to the area as his sheep were.

'Well, I sometimes think of giving up and heading off, but I wonder if I've left it too late. It's a big economic upheaval to do that.'

I had been hoping of course that he'd tell me he loved being in the hills and could never ever give them up. But the truth is harsher. His was a small, tenanted farm. A single Herdwick sheep costs about seventy-five pence to shear and the fleece will make ten pence at market. It is a lot of work to shear a sheep, but it has to be done. If bad weather comes, the upland farmer has to prepare to go up the mountain to look for problems, not like the tourist, running for home. When it snows, there will be feed to be taken up there. The 2001 foot and mouth outbreak took a terrible toll. The flocks were culled with a savage and ruthless efficiency. Re-establishing flocks which would settle on their own patch of hill had been a complicated task.

Walking with Tony, Bess, Jed and Laddie and a flock of 100 Herdwick sheep had introduced me to a series of wonderful interlocking traditions. But I could see that the agricultural landscape was gradually becoming as much of a museum as Dove Cottage. It makes little economic sense to continue to farm this way. We may be preserving the countryside that inspired Wordsworth, and it is a gorgeous, gorgeous thing, but it will become increasingly expensive. These hills really are a garden. How long will we be prepared to tend it with no return?

Wordsworth believed that Lakeland created a special race of people. He described it as 'an almost visionary mountain republic'. Before him, Thomas Gray had called the Lakes 'a little mountain paradise' and in the 1790s John Housman, a local boy, was moved enough to describe 'a happy people, who inhabit the peaceful dales shut up in the mountains'. They were 'the pure emanation of nature and honesty'. It was as if the hills themselves bred wonderful independent 'modest, unaffected and humble' folk. It just shows what lovely scenery can do. A little further north, where the hills were a little more challenging, the place apparently thronged with 'bloodthirsty highland savages'.

Much of this special grace actually derived from the way land was owned, by 'statesmen' with large, independent farms, rather than tenants on big aristocratic estates. It sounds like an echo of Rousseau's open admiration for the Swiss Cantons and their democracies. And these hill folk were also the sort of people who were drawn to new religious movements.

I wandered a little out of the National Park to visit Briggflatts, in the former county of Westmorland. It was a very early Quaker meeting house, and a building worth sitting in silently for half an hour – whitewashed on the outside and stone-walled on the inside, with a bare and beautiful unornamented meeting room, surrounded by an upper gallery of pews. A few burnt-orange flowers in a vase on a central table, a flash of gold, were the only real decoration. It was a reminder that the puritan taste is also the modern taste. It was the sort of room that was built for contemplation, and that was what I was here to do.

The Friends had assembled so that we could have a meeting (not a service) and they were serving soup and sandwiches to a noisy and enthusiastic, perfectly ordinary-looking bunch of people as we arrived. Then we went into the room and arranged ourselves around the pews. Quiet is the essential starting point of a Quaker meeting. Friends sit together and commune without talking. No priest guides them. They open their minds and allow the ministry of the Lord to come to them. They do not expect there to be a leader. Each person is equal in the sight of God.

'How do you stop thinking about the shopping?' I asked later.

'I don't, but that soon goes,' Carole explained.

Some closed eyes. A child played with a toy and whispered a bit. Otherwise a sort of restfulness settled on the room. I kept thinking of when I had been a choirboy and was expected to sit, kneel and pray in the local church. The short

moments of silence had seemed very long then, and I had fidgeted. But I was older now. The motes danced in the light, the sound of breathing was calming. I became rather attracted to this form of worship, a process that somehow brought the rushing world to a stop for a bit, and required participants to meditate not on their own, but collectively.

After about five minutes it was actually Tim, our camera assistant, who stood for the first ministry. 'I'm sorry to interrupt...' he announced in precise, well-modulated tones from the upper balcony, '...but the police are worried about the parking.'

We settled the cars and then it was back to silence.

Two women finally spoke – quoting psalms – and mindful of our mission, I suppose, they talked of the inspiration of hills and the presence of God in them. Then two ladies shook hands and the meeting was over.

The Friends have faith in the word of the Bible and a strong commitment to the ideals of modesty and peace. 'What is it that you believe, then?' I asked, rather boldly, afterwards.

'As Jesus said, "I just know,"' Roy Stephenson replied. (He had helped organize this meeting for us.) 'We actually have atheist Quakers and humanist Quakers among the Friends.'

It is pretty widely acknowledged that the Quaker movement was founded in the hills not far from Briggflatts. So Roy took me up there. I was expecting the site of this important meeting to be dramatic, and it was, but, like the Quakers themselves, in a subtle and undemonstrative way.

A 'serious young man' called George Fox, during the disruptions of the English Revolution of 1688, had come to question the power and methods of the established Church. Reading his Bible, now in English of course, George became convinced that it was time to get back to the true teaching of Christ. He set off on a grand tour of the countryside speaking his mind and God's word. He was arrested by magistrates in Derby for blasphemy. He told the court that he recognized only the authority of God, not of man, and recommended that his examiners themselves should tremble in the presence of the Lord. As a result they labelled him 'the Quaker', though personally George always preferred the rather Marc Bolan-ish appellation 'Child of Light'. Today many Quakers call themselves 'Friends'.

ABOVE: Briggflatts.
BELOW: Sitting in silence at a Quaker meeting and thinking about the shopping.

Fox had had 'a vision of a great multitude waiting to be gathered' and on Firbank Fell he finally got one. In this windswept spot he preached that God could speak directly to man to a host of about 1000 people, drawn to him out of the surrounding fields. The movement was born.

Did the spirit of the Friends owe anything to the geography of the mountains?

Firbank Fell held little more than a cemetery, a wall and a couple of bent trees. A narrow road ran south straight down a long, long hill. We had to move our cars around to let people pass. It was a bare, open landscape. The mountains were only distant presences, their peaks adding miles to the sense of horizon. This was a place of wind and bent grass and whale-backed hills. We were clearly high. There was a far glint of a town right off and beyond, but there was none of the enclosing cosiness of the central Lakes out here.

Even today the famous Cumbrian independence, and the no-nonsense, let's-not-make-a-fuss, we're-each-as-good-as-each-other Westmorland stance, must have their origins in what is actually a tough pragmatic landscape. This is still good Quaker territory. The hills do seem to breed decent, thoughtful folk.

Lesley and Sarah worked in the Fred Holdsworth Bookshop in Ambleside. It was delightfully cramped. One entire wall was covered with mountain books and guides. While we filmed, they made us tea. They were a double act. One wrapped, one took the money. They sat behind the till on stools of different heights, smiling at me and watching me burrow in their mountain section.

What a lot of mountain books there are. The Lake poets may have written the manual, but people still seem to get inspired by them hills, though I have to say that most of it appears to be of an assault-and-battery level – 'Up Into The Empty Challenge Against the Odds Beyond the Threatening Endurance – Alone', where the cliffs tower and the empty air defies adjectives. I do it myself. There's plenty of my own struggle for the heights in here, of course. Just like everybody else I wanted to keep a record of my thrills. I remember when *Touching the Void* was my bedtime reading and my poor wife thought I was ill. 'What are you groaning about?'

'He's fallen into the crevice and broken both his legs beneath the knees.'

Then, three minutes later,

'Stop groaning.'

'Sorry. He's decided to crawl home.'

When I started this programme I wanted to remain resistant to all those notions of 'assault', 'conquering', 'triumph' and 'struggle', but as you clamber up to the highest peaks it becomes part of the vocabulary. Climbing is awfully self-centred. I wonder how many of the hard nuts who write the more strenuous books ever really stop to consider the view, unless it's a frightening one.

The Lakeland mountains seem to offer a gentler perspective. Somewhere between the park and Anapurna tramps the fell walker and his stout boots. And the champion of their philosophy is Alfred Wainwright. He wrote a series of guides to the Lakes that has gathered a following as dedicated as Wordsworth's.

He undoubtedly has a cult status here in Ambleside. The little matching volumes with their primary-coloured sleeves are laid out in a sequence that covers every single fell and dale in the Lakes. They were written between 1952 and 1966, entirely from personal experience. I admired the handsome wrapper and flipped through the pages. It's like a missal – a monkish illustrated diary – or perhaps a rather beautiful school geography project. There is not a sliver of print on show.

ABOVE: Alfred Wainwright's beautiful school geography project guidebook.

The words are entirely handwritten, to squeeze neatly in between the maps, the hand-drawn illustrations of the views and the ink drawings of objects encountered on the way. He even hand-lettered the publisher's name. In order to make it all fit, he would adjust his language, using a short word if a long one took up too much space and expanding a thought to fill the space if required. So it feels completely and appropriately home-made – as if you are carrying a work of art around.

It's a good series for bookshops. The uniform edition is very collectable. You have to have the set. Just in case. Lesley agreed. 'And, of course, the one you take out gets damp and a little ragged, doesn't it?'

'So it's proper to buy two,' Sarah added.

But they're not cheap, nor are spin-offs such as *In the Footsteps of Wainwright, Wainwright's Walks – in Photographs, Where Wainwright Trod.* Everybody wants to get on the Wainwright trail.

It was a club that I resisted a little to begin with, but on closer examination I could see that the books deserve their reputation. Like all good finds they are something you want to be a personal discovery. Ironically, the direct copies of his technique – pamphlets with dotted paths and notes in somebody else's handwriting – only show how brilliant Wainwright was, because the rivals are too coarse. Wainwright's pernickety precision is reassuring. Like the name 'Wainwright', the books have a sturdy Lancastrian utility about them. They have a craftsmanship; an obsessive, painstaking application. They are redolent of good boots or hand-pulled beer or paraffin lights. They are something practical and well-made – and almost became as difficult to get hold of.

Given their following, it is surprising that they nearly went out of print. They were originally put out by the local newspaper, and then moved to a proper grown-up publisher, but recently it nearly decided to discontinue them. The reason for this is that they were getting redundant as proper usable guides. Wainwright himself had never wanted to update them. The original task was enough for one man. Their style was so individual and so idiosyncratic, who could ever reproduce it?

A determined soul called Chris Jesty has stepped forward. I met him in a car park to step further forward with him myself, on one of Wainwright's walks up Catbells. It was a good choice, because it seems the epitome of the Wainwright approach. 'Words cannot adequately describe the rare charm of Catbells,'

Wainwright wrote. He identified it as a 'family fell, where grandmothers and infants can climb the heights together'. And with that you sense the man's affection for the Lake District. He was not so very interested in conquest and challenge. He wanted to walk, to explore and most of all to enjoy, and he did so in his second-best, straightforward tweed suit.

Chris was wearing his own tweed suit and plus-fours to boot, or not quite to boot. They stopped, as plus-fours should, just below his knees, at natty yellow socks which disappeared into good leather lace-up boots. He was wearing a tie. I felt ashamed of my 'engineered' outdoor wear and shiny anorak.

The rain had stopped. There were a few red sails slipping across Derwentwater. We climbed steeply up from the bushy lane through waist-high bracken, with Chris already making notes in his edition. The car park had moved. The main

ABOVE: Catbells and the red sails on Derwentwater.

access to the fell, as marked by Wainwright, had shifted with it. We stood for a moment at a crossroads, a couple of hundred yards along the path, and took our bearings. Chris did this literally. He carried not just one GPS system, but three. Two were needed for cross-referencing. 'They can fail, you see. They are by no means as accurate as people believe.' The third was a spare, in case the other two broke. This was the sort of belt and braces approach that Wainwright himself would have approved of. Here was the obsessiveness of the master. Chris made notes of the directions of the new paths and the point where they joined. A few small changes and some satellite observations to mark the exact positions and the guide would be usable again.

As we walked on, up what was already a busy track, overtaken by student

ABOVE: Chris Jesty checks I'm going the right way up Catbells.

parties, people walking dogs and couples arm in arm, Chris explained that the publisher had set up a computer model of Wainwright's handwriting, so any changes that he needed to make would be invisibly mended. He wasn't there to rewrite the guides, just to make slightly more accurate readings for the maps and to note the major alterations.

This was reassuring. We came to our first stony section and clambered over a few rocks heading up to the first of the bells. 'There is beauty everywhere – and nothing but beauty,' Wainwright had written. At the summit, like a bald head, surmounted by a pate of rock, the guidebook came into its own. We could stand and use his carefully drawn and labelled vista, hold it at the right angle to the compass and employ it to identify all the fading peaks we could see in the distance. But if directions were everything, these guides would hardly need preserving. There are plenty of other accurate rivals. Wainwright is not merely accurate, he is opinionated. His books are dedicated by turns to dogs and sheep. He passes comments on the sorts of people he meets. He jokes about his own anonymity. He is a completely human companion, who liked fish and chips, was burly but not particularly athletic, and urged people not to look on the fells as enemies to be conquered, but as 'tried and trusted friends, always there when needed'.

Wainwright wrote that, from the top of Catbells, the eye is 'continually drawn to Derwentwater, Keswick and the great fells the other side'. He was right. It was truly difficult to turn and go down that hill. The cottages to the west sat in a perfect valley, an exquisite vision of enfolding green field and hedge trees. To the east the lake glittered in the evening sun. It was faultless landscape and it was a feast. Hungry eyes roamed the undulating hills and the lake shore, devouring detail and gobbling up event. It was precisely because there was so much incident, so many little reminders of human activity perfectly spread out before us, that the intellect was so satisfied. This was the Lakeland of legend. A place that could hardly fail to inspire, if only to take a photograph.

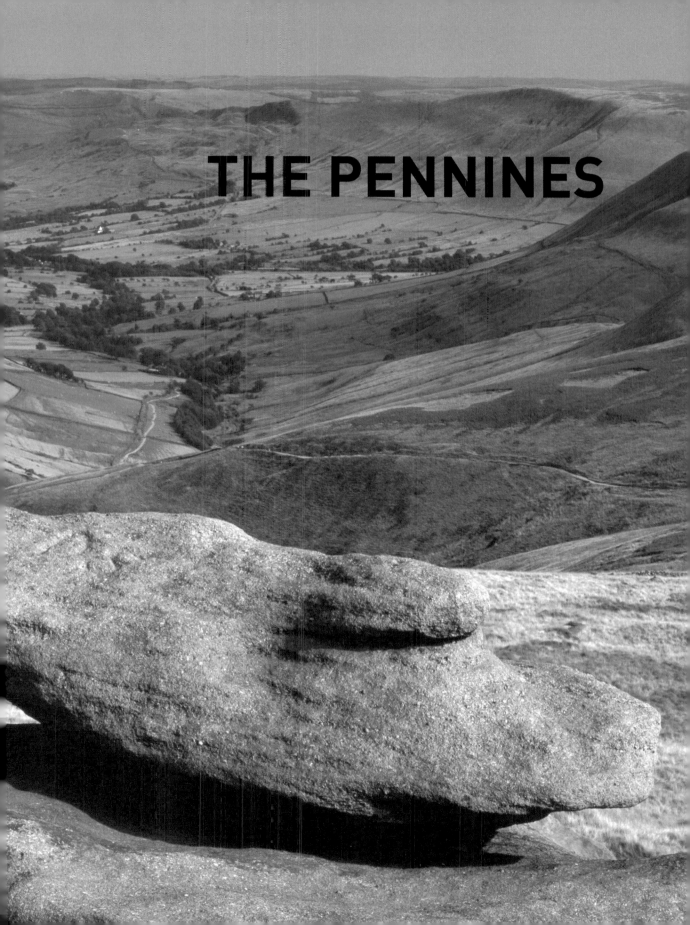

THE PENNINES

CHAPTER FOUR

The Pennines

I arrived in the Pennines by train. Not the West Highland steamer chuffing into Fort William, or the overnight sleeper to Keswick or even the imported Swiss mountain railway, heaving itself up Snowdon. This was an Intercity Express, on a busy mainline route, and it dropped me in the heart of a northern industrial city, ready to start climbing the yellow barriers of Sheffield station.

The Pennines, the backbone of Britain, can hardly deliver clichés about the 'unconquerable roof of the world'. New York stockbrokers don't 'grab a Pennine' for their international peak-challenge scalp belt. As I took my luggage down from the rack I knew I was no longer in the wild. Half of Britain's entire population lives within a yodel of these moderately impressive hillocks.

Other mountains I had 'conquered' influenced Britain because they were on the margin, with populations that were outsiders, but the Pennines are highlands in the back garden. Manchester was just on the other side of that hill. Barnsley, Leeds, Preston and Liverpool were all nearby. Running north for some 160 miles, the Pennines raised a wall between Lancashire and Yorkshire. Could it be much of a barrier? What responsibility did these hills have for the kingmakers of the late Middle Ages, for the growth of the great empires of cotton and steel or for the huge conurbations that grew up on either side of them? How did the people of the towns respond to these hills – use them, play in them, ignore them?

And, after all that, where was the camera exactly?

It's a nervous business descending from a train on film. The director always wants to do it again a few times – 'You know, since the train is actually still waiting in the station, Griff.'

RIGHT: Kinder Downfall. The waterfall was blowing upwards when we were there.

What he really wants is a shot where I slam the door and the train smoothly draws away, in one seamless action. But that means timing. It means fearlessness. It means: 'I can't get this bloody door open!'

With all the whistling and shouting and the panic, the most important thing, apparently, was that I should try to look as unimpressed as I would be if I were really arriving at Sheffield.

George Orwell once wrote that Sheffield could claim to be the ugliest city in the Old World, believing this would please Sheffield, because they liked to be pre-eminent in everything. This was long before the Luftwaffe and the town council got to work.

Like many pub experts, I had assumed that the decline of this city was down to the decline of its steel industry. In fact Sheffield today produces more steel than it did during the Second World War and mostly in new, technically advanced factories that employ few and are 'owned by foreigners'. We hurried through the city, however, to a good old-fashioned workshop. Smoking, clattering and burning, it was reet devilish.

Norton Cast Products Ltd made individual orders for the oil industry in a series of impressive sheds. They mixed their molten goo in huge tubs suspended from the ceiling. While I was waiting to explore I watched as a man stuck a long pole into a white-hot crucible, pulled it out and let liquid metal drip in gobbets on the floor. He twisted the remainder around the end, like toffee on a stick, and I found myself thinking I would quite like to do that.

Everywhere tubs of ingredients were at hand so that these steel founders could add a little more zest, or a pinch more flavouring, to get exactly the product they wanted. Huge gantries and hanging chains carried finished work across a busy floor. An aura of fierce commitment hung over the workshop. The intensity of the heat was matched by the concentration of the foundry workers, who looked like medieval alchemists mixing recipes for gold. This was Vulcan's workshop and the processes used here were quite close to those that made this city pre-eminent in steel.

The 'crucible method', which transformed Sheffield's fortunes, was discovered by a clockmaker, Benjamin Huntsman, in 1740, but the ingredients that made steel came from the hills – the fluorspar, the lime, the iron ore and the coal, and

RIGHT: It's not really a competition. Andy Cave (2nd left) and the kids.

perhaps most importantly, the water. The hills are very wet. The peat sits up on their tops like a giant layer of sponge and collects the rain that flows onto and through the limestone crust, gathering strength as it approaches Sheffield. Here five separate rivers combine, and at one time a thousand watermills ran hammers and dowsed white-hot metal using that power. This busy town and the Pennine mountains were linked by an umbilical cord of water.

They were also linked by good roads. Like many of Britain's big cities, Sheffield doesn't look prosperous at all, except in the suburbs. The centre may have been abused but the outskirts seemed a leafy, well-kept paradise. I whisked through them and out to a foggy lay-by where I had an appointment with a minibus. It came out of the mist like the Flying Dutchman. I climbed in the back. The children from the school I had arranged to go climbing with were all dressed in smart, new, matching beige jackets and bright, yellow boots.

After half an hour's drive we parked and began the walk up to the rock face, chattering about our expectations. Only one of them had been out here before, and done a little climbing with his dad.

Stanage Edge was, for a change, close to the road. It was not a mountain: it was a cliff, as its name implied. About the height of my house, it stretched away into opaque fuzziness, a three-and-a-half-mile broken limestone wall with, apparently, a thousand registered climbs on it. You could easily miss it. Appropriately, given its proximity to Sheffield, it felt like a natural community facility, a serviceable, accessible climbing wall for a large population centre, handily provided by the last ice age.

I had an advantage over the kids in that I had almost climbed two rock faces before. Except for cocky Jordan, they were novices. They had the advantage over me, being generally tiny, fit and fearless. Yes, yes, I know. Who says it wasn't a competition? Jordan thought it was. I just didn't want to disgrace myself, that's all.

Andy Cave was leading us. He had been a miner and when the strike came in the mid-eighties he vented some of his frustration by climbing rocks. (His boyhood hobby – scaling electricity pylons – came in useful.) Now he took groups of city kids for their first adventure. Yesterday he had visited the school and told them the story of how he went to sleep, in a tent, on a ledge, several thousand feet up a rock face. The ledge fell off, so he woke up tied to nothing but his tent. They had been impressed. He didn't have anything to prove. He could just stand in front of a cliff and point out the various footholds like a gym teacher showing them the wall bars.

Natalie was to go ahead of me. The stone was like a wrinkled dishcloth. It broke into weird, smoothed shapes with a sculptural complexity heightened by the white mist. This was natural Giacometti, innate Henry Moore. (Moore actually used to go up on to the Yorkshire hills to seek inspiration from weathered stone like this.) Some of the slab – a big, three-room section – had clearly split and fallen in some previous erosion and lay carelessly propped up against the remaining cliff. This was what Natalie shinned up now. She was roped from above and easily found enough protrusions in the stone to pull herself onwards. If she couldn't quite do it she giggled and waited for instruction. Marvellous. I would have been crying and blaming everyone.

But of course as I watched I began to think it looked simple. Yes, I could manage that. It always happened when somebody did something smoothly. It's one of the great spurs to recklessness. Natalie made it look very easy.

It was my turn. I had my funny ballet shoes on. I had to get a few fingers on to a half-inch nodule and heave. Close to, and actually grabbing it, the seemingly organic and cushion-like gritstone was unyielding. The lumps were smoothed by water erosion and my fingers slipped and bruised as I scrabbled to get a grip. It hurt just to hold on. Rock is hard and, though Ollie down below was pulling me up, there was no sense that anyone could fall with impunity. Slip and a nasty bang threatened. Seen from below the wall sloped. It became vertical as I clambered. Once I mounted the cliff the people down below became tiny very quickly. As I looked down from the first ledge, they seemed much smaller than Natalie had appeared looking up at her.

I'm sure there shouldn't have been, but there was a lot of scrabbling and pushing and scraping, along with a considerable amount of tightening of the chest and

ABOVE: Stanage Edge. Not for the International Peak Challenge Scalp Belt but handy for Sheffield.

audible breathing, before I finally got over the last, Ford Focus-sized ledge and stood on my slightly quivering legs again. Everybody politely applauded and I blushed.

It doesn't take much to belittle the Pennines. 'A bracing walk for the dog, a fun park for kids, a nice place to stick a few reservoirs.' After leaving the school climbers and taking the long road southwards out of Sheffield, I stopped by an exquisite village nestling in a cleft in the Peak Park. Not many mountains here: to a Tibetan mere sleeping policemen. But in Britain we have the Countryside & Rights of Way Act of 2000, which helpfully defines a mountain as an area of land above 600 metres in height. Along the 160-mile length of the Pennines there is plenty of such high land.

ABOVE: Looking for nodules on a wrinkled dishcloth.

To get around the huge lateral distances, I had a camper van. A new generation finds the Volkswagen sleeper redolent of hip sixties Californian grooviness; to me, it was an old van. But this one had been given a World of Interiors make-over. It had Damien Hirst spotty curtains and cushions. It had a concertina roof that pushed up to give extra headroom. Even the stove unfolded. There was no power steering, though, so this camper van really, really required driving, if not positively motivating. The gear stick was a two-foot knitting needle with a knob on, or sometimes with a knob off. And the exact whereabouts of the gate was a matter of sensitive experiment. I could sit at a junction for hours trying to perfect the art of inserting a sausage into a bridge roll with a two-foot wire.

Other motorists were so enchanted by my vehicle's retro chic that they formed long queues behind to get a good look at it. (Or, who knows, perhaps they just wanted to overtake me.) This was appropriate, though. Before the Industrial Revolution the raw materials that were to be found in these mountains were carted about in the pre-industrial equivalent of my camper van. They could take days to cross the hills. I went up to look at a packhorse trail and temporarily swapped my VW for Tyson, the wonder horse.

I sensed that Tyson knew I had spent four years cursing my daughter's equine obsession. Horses are not forgiving animals. What on earth do horsey people and members of the royal family find to get so affectionate about? I only see an over-large quadruped with rolling eyeballs, huge, yellow teeth and unhealthy quivers of distrust rippling through its powerful body.

Living up to his name, Tyson was a monster and, as we all know, utterly harmless. I had to practise in an indoor school. Here he plodded round placidly enough, but that was only because everybody was watching him. Out on the packhorse trail he quickly reverted.

'This is the old route to Rochdale,' I pronounced from my mount. 'If we move just up there we can see that the path is still cobbled with stones, which were laid to enable the horse to get a grip through the more difficult territory.'

I kicked Tyson on. He stayed where he was. I flicked at the reins in an encouraging manner but firmly enough to show him that I was in control. Ha! Tyson was indomitable. He was placid all right. He was marmoreal. He stood there like a stuffed horse on a plinth, while I poked him, patted him, cajoled

him and kicked him. 'Hah! Hey! Hup! Ho!'

'Let's just go again,' said the director. He was rolling his eyes as manically as Tyson now.

So I uttered the deathless words again, and again did that 7th Cavalry thing, where they jerk the whole body in the saddle. Tyson was a very big horse – sixteen hands. He gave the same reaction that he might have given if an infant mouse had gone 'Hah!' and jerked purposefully about on his back. He stood implacably and breathed heavily. Then he started going backwards. Even the camper van never did that.

We were joined by an expert horsewoman, Christine Peat, who was capably riding her own white mare – so capably in fact that if Tyson chose to go backwards she could make her horse go backwards too. She tutted at Tyson. She scolded him, but, between you and me, I got the impression that she was probably thinking, poor Tyson, being ridden by such a jillock. I know she was. That's what horsey people think.

Christine had been instrumental in reopening some of the old packhorse ways, which generally still operated as footpaths and were traceable from their names. 'The route that carried salt passed through towns that took their home from the trade, like Salford,' Christine told me. 'Lime-carriage resulted in "Lymington" and so on.'

Packhorses were the HGVs of their day. They carried a lot more than ribbons and fancy goods. Lead mined in these hills was taken away in baskets, two to a horse, and each horse was capable of carrying up to sixteen stone. They could make about fifteen miles a day and then they needed a special resting place: inns with gigantic stables, where numerous trains could rest the night. The restorers of these trails were themselves setting up a chain of inns with facilities for keeping horses, so, like backpackers or camper-vanners, the horse-hiker could take off and follow the paths for days at a time, wherever their horse would carry them.

I learned all this riding backwards down a hill.

Clearly I would have needed one of these inns every hundred yards. When Tyson wasn't gradually edging home he seemed to have fallen into equine catatonia. He flicked his tail and admired the view. It was a good view. Across the valley were the remains of old mines, below that a railway and alongside

ABOVE: The camper van struggles with a death-defying slight incline.
BELOW: Tyson successfully ignores the orange peanut on his back.

this a busy trunk road – industry, commerce and communication, all in one sweeping vista.

'Why are we, on the packhorse trail, so far up the hillside?' I asked.

Christine explained that the valleys had been so boggy, and the slopes such good hideouts for bandits, that the trails had always stayed on the uplands, not right on the top but just in the lee of the hill, where they could shelter from blizzards. For a true horseman with a trusting mount, following these high trails across the peaks would now be an ideal way to see the Pennines. For me it was back to the camper van. I still had to explore more of this great northern barrier – going forwards if possible.

I met Inspector Philip Bromley at a police station just round the back of a service station on the M62, sitting in his regulation Day-Glo Range Rover. Phil was a scion of a family business – his father had been a policeman and so was his brother. We cruised steadily along the highest motorway in Britain, before coming off at one of those secret-looking, reserved parking places. From here we climbed up to what must be the most commanding police car lookout point in the whole of Great Britain. Set on a concrete escarpment with several big metal poles sticking out of the flanks, it stood a good fifty feet above the road.

'It's something to do with the drainage,' Phil explained. 'The lads call it the Guns of Navarone.'

Our eyrie was undoubtedly the work of the navvies, imported on to the wild moorland to build the road. They had camped up here among the heather and a special 'house of comfort' had been built for them. There was a scandal when the police came and closed it down; not because it was a brothel but because, outrageously, it had taken to serving drink without a liquor licence.

From where we sat we had a superb view of the highest motorway in Britain. The M62 was built straight across Saddleworth Moor, where Brady and Hindley buried their victims. It passed directly under the Pennine Way, which had been lifted incongruously on to a cantilevered cat's cradle of a bridge, dead ahead of us, and ran down the other side of the summit to Sheffield and Leeds, carrying a hundred thousand cars a day.

Modern engines barely register the incline. We hardly imagine such a hill is any

RIGHT: Saddleworth Moor.

obstacle at all. We were, after all, no more than a thousand feet above 'normal'. But when the snow came it could drift across the road, making it impassable, and then the police had to shut the whole motorway.

'People don't expect it,' Phil explained. 'It's a busy link between two big cities and some drivers don't like it. We have to chase people in 4x4s who move the barriers and set off regardless.'

Personally I was rather impressed. I liked the idea that the mountain could bite back. Before providing the resources that started the Industrial Revolution, that built these cities and this great road, the Pennines had also been the barrier between two rival peoples. Just in front of us was the county border. Six hundred years ago the House of Lancaster had been set against the House of York. The resultant War of the Roses had wandered all over the country, with battles as far away as London,

but the rivalry between Lancastrians and Yorkshiremen is still legendary and I had been promised a taste of the Pennine divide at a ladies' darts match in the highest pub in England, the Tan Hill Inn.

These were serious girls, because county darts is a serious game. I sensed a slight, and I mean just the merest dusting, of frost in the pub, when I stomped in out of the freezing night. The Yorkshire team, though dressed in matching white T-shirts by request of the television crew, had not expected the Lancashire team to field their actual county players, let alone turn up in full bright-red county regalia.

Yorkshire were frankly a little embarrassed, with the pursed lips and edginess that comes from the realization that the opposite side are not treating 'a friendly' with quite the comradely insouciance expected. And, though everyone was very matey, the two teams definitely kept to their own. Lancashire were, to be frank, just a little more eager in virtually every department.

'So is it true that Yorkshire can be a little, what shall I say, close with their money?' I ventured carefully.

'Oh, good lord, yes. Mean as anything, that lot.'

I blinked.

'They can't cook!'

'No sense of humour. There's no fun in them.'

The catalogue of county failings rattled out.

'Bad losers.'

'Think they own the earth.'

'Oh, snooty – you're dead right there.'

'Ladies! Ladies!' I could hardly stop them as they all piled in. So I bought everyone a drink and scurried across to the Yorkshire girls.

They were a trifle disconcerted. 'Did they say that?'

'Yes.'

'Well, that's typical for a start.'

The lasses exchanged wary glances.

'Are you mean, then? Do you think?'

'We're good, down-to-earth folk. We don't go flashing it around like they do, if

LEFT: Lancashire get ready for the contest by placing me directly in front of the dartboard.

that's what you're implying.'

I changed the subject. We talked instead about their chances in the game, but it was time to step up to the oche.

There was a tension in the air. Not quite the tension that accompanied the matches between the two counties in national competitions, attended by crowds of thousands in Blackpool, but enough to merit considerable celebrations when Lancashire finally won, with a neat double three. Afterwards the red-shirted roses gathered round the table by the window and started to sing:

'Lancashire leads the way, Lancashire leads the way.

Whatever they do in London, we did it yesterday,

Lancashire, Lancashire,

Lancashire leads the way, hey.'

So at least, as a Londoner, I was marginally more backward than a Yorkshireman.

By the middle of the next morning I had travelled further north into the Yorkshire hills and was looking at the entrance to a lead mine. It was neat and unexpectedly discreet, like a miniature railway tunnel. A nicely dressed arch of stone, almost hidden away in a bank, stood above a metal-barred gate. A constant stream of water flowed from the entrance at ground level. It looked pure and clean, but this was not always the case. Sometimes the water was so sulphurous and acidic that it burned away the workers' boots.

How many tunnels and shafts looped and burrowed into the hills? The entrance didn't go down, because the hills were so thick. It drove straight forward, at the minimum height necessary to access the seams of lead, with railway lines running up the middle through the water.

The work of getting trucks of ore out of this mine must have been back-breaking. Just to enter the mine necessitated bending double. The entrance would have been perfect for Snow White's seven dwarves, for these were ancient mines with a whiff of legend about them. It was half a mile beyond here that the grid of shafts and tunnels started in earnest, as the workings followed the lead. Tons of rock and stone had had to be smashed, crushed and cleared away to get at the lode-bearing seams. The best and easiest pickings had now been taken. All that

remained was the mine itself, a mill wheel and the visitor centre.

Jimmy Craggs had worked in the mines until the eighties. He was there to show me one of the prize exhibits in the museum – his spar box. Mostly dating from the Victorian period, spar boxes are landscapes, fantasies and scenes constructed in cabinets, out of 'the bonnie bits', mineral crystals discovered by the miners during their work.

'They were just there,' Jim told me. 'In lough holes. We'd be working with the drill and the bit would go in, like, and give, and you'd think, aye, aye, I've got one here.'

The drill bit had sunk into a natural bubble formed by the cooling processes of the rock in its volcanic stage and there in the darkness, over millions of years, mineral crystals had grown.

ABOVE: Closely examining 'the bonnie bits' that make up the crazy landscape of a spar box.

'We weren't supposed to take them, you see,' said Jim. 'Strictly, like, everything in the mine belonged to the owners, but the foremen would turn a blind eye and we'd put the goodies in our pockets. It were one of the perks.'

They could have sold them. There are plenty of mineral collectors. These crystals are not exactly gems, but the specimens on display on the first floor of the museum would have given even Elizabeth Taylor palpitations. Each one was a different crystalline compound, some growing in alien geometric shapes, some glistening with dustings of pyrites. Oddly, as the labels revealed, in the beginning they were regarded as worthless, except as specimens, but later it seemed industrial uses were found for all of them. All, in their way, became valuable items. Fluorspar, the green one, and certainly the most common, began to be mined in its own right, for use in the manufacture of steel. Other compounds were used in the manufacture of Teflon or toothpaste, or were important in the production of rubber or aluminium.

Jim told me about his finest discovery, when his bit dropped right through the rock into what he assumed must be a gigantic lough hole. Indeed it proved to be big enough to walk into. 'It was covered all over the interior with the stuff – all over.'

'So was it dusty?'

'No, no. It was clean. Dead clean.'

There was something eerie about such riches, so much useful material, lying beneath these hills. Not only the obvious metals, but all the other chemicals necessary for the working of those metals. All had been created by the huge forces that had formed the Earth's crust.

But even more discombobulating is the idea that it is now cheaper and easier to drag the stuff out of pits miles beneath the surface of distant countries, and transport it here, than it is to continue to exploit the deposits in our own backyard. In fact this trend took root almost from the beginning of the industrial process.

The first mines were carved out up in the hills because the hills were broken and so allowed access to seams. Heavy industry continued in this region for centuries. Fluorspar is still mined, but not lead. The stuff that Jimmy pocketed to make his spar box, then virtually worthless to the owner, is now the only business in the hills.

I leaned forward in order to peer into the cold darkness of the spar boxes. Most of them were formed into crystal landscapes, with strange crystal trees that could have been the surfaces of planets as imagined by Victorians. The most famous, the Eggleston box, however, was as tall as me and displayed a street, encrusted with glittering stones and lit by a Narnia-like lamppost. Using an ingenious arrangement of mirrors, the street stretched away into a frightening and surreal townscape, De Chirico-like and empty – a cold, moonlit, jewel-encrusted dream.

Jim's own box was rather more homely. It was the only one got up to look like a mine. He had concentrated almost entirely on green stones, some a shocking emerald colour. It depicted two men working away on separate levels, each gradually digging out a chamber, exactly as they would have done, except that every inch of the wall glittered with green crystal.

I liked it very much and told Jim so.

'Do you want to buy it then?' he asked.

Nenthead mine and its heritage centre, where Jim and I met, were tucked away under a stand of thick, unnatural Forestry Commission fir trees, a strange and muffling new growth, utterly and completely enfolding. It was impenetrable and uniform compared with what lay beyond – what seemed to be miles of hilly, deserted, windswept nothing. But when I looked closer I could see that the area all around was scored and pitted and heaped with slews of slag, much of this now overgrown with grass.

David Walker Barker was an artist-in-residence at the heritage centre and had built several artworks based on the ideas of the spar boxes. 'It is a palimpsest,' he told me as we stood together looking over this spare landscape, our blue hands buried in our pockets. 'This is like layers of hidden text about the relationship of man and the land beneath.'

In Wales the slate mines still ravage the hills, looking like recent wounds. But here the workings seemed long dead, muted and blanketed. Whitened scars. To build his own boxes David had had to search hard for the residue of the mining days, scraps from a life that had now gone – rusty bits of metal, old, opaque grey-glass bottles, bits of a child's broken shoe and a bleached skull.

It was a freezing evening with a biting wind and a bright-blue interplanetary sky. Everything was sharp and unreal. As we stood talking the sun set behind the hill and the cold deepened. There was beauty here, but it wasn't the kindly, reassuring beauty of the Lake District, just a few miles away to the west. It provided a different inspiration. Deeply scarred and rather dour, this was a landscape where men had struggled. It was very Yorkshire and very Pennine.

The next morning it was still almost dark when we checked into the Pen-y-Ghent café for the Yorkshire Three Peaks Challenge. These peaks are amongst the highest mountains in the Pennine range and are its main claim to be included in any survey of British mountains. Pen-y-Ghent rises 694 metres, Ingleborough 723 and Whernside 736. All of them are great, step-sided slabs of hill made of alternating layers of limestone and gritstone with a bit of shale thrown in. They were laid down as a series of sea bottoms about 350 million years ago and then raised up six million years ago. This is limestone territory and the stuff has startling effects on the landscape.

The Challenge is now so famous that hundreds go for it. At the café there is a clocking-in machine. You take a card, write your name, address and telephone number on it, punch it in an old factory timer and then hand it over the counter for safe keeping. It is important to return and clock out. I suppose people could be forgiven for thinking, as they get back to the car park, 'Oh never mind, it took too long, we don't need a record of it,' but for the café this is more than a game. Fail to come back and the staff alert the rescue services, but only after they themselves have chewed their fingernails and pulled out their hair for hours. For one man they stayed until three in the morning. He is a university lecturer and still returns to order a cup of tea in one of their huge mugs, and boast about his status as the man they waited up all night for.

I had already discovered, though, that most ramblers are responsible. When they come back they clock out. It's the old story of this unexpectedly dangerous sport – one that still claims lives every year. You have to have some self-discipline to get as far as the café, more to get past the first stile and a lot to start up the stony cliff.

The guidebook tells you you're not going to beat any records, because the Three Peaks is a well-known hill race. The shortest times are around two and half hours. While I was waiting I looked at the pictures of the fell runners who come in the summer to do it. They are a separate breed too, with none of the honed, quivering, race-horse look of champion marathon runners. The grainy black-and-white pictures showed sturdy farmers in loose vests with round, flushed Yorkshire faces and Bobby Charlton hairdos, some of them of indeterminate age. That meant they might even have been my age, though I guessed they were ten years younger.

The companions for my ascent were certainly a lot younger than me. They were

RIGHT: The Pennines rise to the occasion at Pen-y-Ghent.

all trainees from the military college at Harrogate. The Army uses the Pennines for fitness training. Robbo (Staff Sergeant Robertson) had picked a special few to try to crack a good time. He was aiming for six or seven hours. They came from all over England, from Plymouth and Hampshire and Newcastle, and were wearing army boots and carrying heavy packs. In a few months they would be signing up to a regiment and probably off to Iraq or Afghanistan. For them fitness was an essential part of survival.

Beginning in broad, green-walled fields, climbing stiles and gates, we set off up the hill at a trot, heading for the stony side of the mountain proper, where the route became the familiar natural staircase. We clambered over piles of boulders and cascades of stone. Sudden waves of competitive enthusiasm would rush through the group as we came near to a wall. The pace would quicken. I needed more breath. The boys on either side would start jostling to be first. Not pushing, just stiffening the pace a little. Like a fool I gave way. 'No, you first.' And by the time I had clambered up the wall I noticed that the leaders had yomped on. Then I needed extra effort to keep up with the group, but this meant doubling my speed or trailing impossibly at the next gate.

Robbo gave me a look; his eyebrow raised a little. This was a test. It was even a test for him.

These lads were seventeen-year-olds with lanky, adolescent frames. I began to wish for longer legs, though I noticed that when we got to the steeper, stony mountainside I was just that little bit steadier. You may think, this man is fooling himself, but my fat thighs, Welsh bottom and recent televised punishment on Ben Nevis ('I'm a celebrity, get me off this mountain') had done me a bit of good here. I could hear laboured panting around me. The fable of hare and tortoise went through my mind. Yes, I was that leathery old tortoise. Ha!

And then we were at the top, in well under an hour, pushing on along a slighter, broad, brown path that passed through yellow, uncropped grass towards the flatter rump of Pen-y-Ghent. A serene, weathered, seemingly endless drystone wall, which had looped up from the valley and twisted a little to take in the verticals, now ran alongside us, stretching across the summit and into the distance.

The park authorities had made, by a stile, a little self-conscious snaky 's' in this wall, but other than that the thing was a fabulous, uncompromising intrusion into a landscape that now soared away on all sides to distant hills and faint echoes of sea. A great, messy weather system was blowing in from the south-west, seemingly no more than a few feet above our heads.

This is where I deserted. Having done my One Peak Challenge, I resigned my commission and baled out. We said our goodbyes. The boys were just as contained as when I met them – a little wary of being caught out – and addressing me as if I was some elderly senior ranker. Almost straight away they started off down the hill towards the distant peak of Ingleborough. Admittedly, having got rid of the tortoise, they actually broke out into a fast trot. Later they told me that the bottom of the valley ahead had been a nightmare of bog and tussock, where more than one of them lost a boot. But I should have done it. I should have proved myself. I had carefully negotiated with the producers for no more than a taste of the event ('You won't want to film me tramping for seven hours!'). I had paraded a series of sensible arguments in a slightly deranged manner. But now I wanted to stay with my group.

Instead I went back to the café and clocked out. After choosing a new and exemplarily silly hat from their impressive stock I set off to walk on a nearby limestone pavement.

LEFT: Staff Sergeant Robbo measures my man boobs.

As pavement goes, it was not much rougher than a lot of Camden Town. But it was one of the wonders of what is known as a karst landscape. Limestone consists of the bones of millions of sea animals. When the rain falls it dissolves the lime and creates an acid that cuts away more stone as it soaks into fissures and cracks. On the high plateaux of the Pennines the rainfall is so constant that in places all the soil has been eroded. A layer of stone has been revealed and the acid has worn furrows, pots, basins and channels out of the clints, or blocks. At the top of grass rises are large areas, sometimes acres in extent, of this fluid hard surface, an organic, groovy, 1960s trelliswork of loopy, surrealist stone. Look down into the holes and you see ferns and glossy-green, orchidaceous things growing there – bloody cranesbill, scabious, rock rose and early purple orchids.

It hardly comes as a surprise that English Nature is on hand, but I had no idea that it was such a unique habitat. 'This is our own rainforest,' Paul Evans pointed out to me as we sat in the midst of this Yorkshire moonscape. 'It exists here because of the rain and is reproduced like this nowhere in the world.' And half of the British stock is here in the Yorkshire Dales.

We were sitting in the middle of what had once been a drovers' route. Thousands of cattle had gone to serve the huge cities at the bottom of the Pennines. They had been replaced by sheep in the past forty years, but sheep, unlike cattle, eat anything, including the rare, lime-loving plants that grow in the hollows. English Nature was experimenting to see if some form of cattle-herding could be reintroduced to help preserve the habitat. They owned the land we were on.

Bill Grayson was their tenant and a keen ecologist himself. He managed the herd of Blue Grey cows that were now eyeing us nervously. They were lovely animals. I am still suburban enough to find cows rather miraculous. Bill was very keen on them too and visited them every day, though they were hardy and independent cattle. That was why they were being reintroduced to the area.

'The truth was that, to begin with, other farmers didn't really want to know. This isn't a big experiment,' Bill explained, 'but it is an example. Now that others see that it can work and it could be productive, then they'll follow.'

'Like sheep.'

'Like Blue Grey cattle.'

Bill rattled his bag of feed and the cows stopped their placid disarrangement

RIGHT: Yorkshire limestone pavement (in better repair than parts of Camden Town).

and vaguely swivelled about until, after a little while, it was noticeable that they were all facing in our direction. He made a high, yipping noise.

'Is that your call?' I asked, hoping that, as with sheep dogs, the language of the cowherd was handed down from a long-lost Viking source.

Bill had to stop and think about this for a while, before asking, 'What did I do?'

'A sort of yip-yip.'

'Yes…' He didn't look entirely impressed. 'I think it's just something I made up. I need some noise to get them. Any sound will do. Here they come.'

The curious cows were jostling up a little slope in the bank, gathering speed as they came. For the benefit of the camera we tried to walk along, chatting about the policy and its effects, which were indeed already plain to see, but the cows were frisky and started nudging us. We quickened our step. They broke into a trot. Here in Ingleborough we were in our own little Pamplona cow run.

'They're quite active,' Bill said.

This is the big appeal of this type of beast. They wear shaggy coats, not so much Highland Angus hippy as dignified elderly theatre director – a swirl of long but thin hair of a lustrous blue-grey. I'm sure it was a rinse, in fact, rather similar to the one my granny used to get at Tonio's.

Twelve other farmers are now joining this scheme. Sophie Grigson has been recruited to – perish the thought – cook some of the cattle. Apparently it is delicious, though I hesitated, cosseted gourmet that I am, to make the connection between these frisky, tinted vegetarians and tasty beef on the table.

But, as we walked back to the little farm, not so much in the shadow of the hills as plonked down on a vast, swirling plain, it seemed extraordinary that the appearance of such an unbounded, open place was so dependent on the relationship between human beings and a few animals. But I could see now that this was a man-made landscape.

Originally the empty, scoured valleys were clothed with trees. Over thousands of years the demand for land and food had stripped every scrap of big vegetation from the view. English Nature was expending a lot of effort to intervene on the side of flowers and butterflies. Some of the lumbering beasts I was leaving behind even wore radio-controlled collars. But farming is still in flux. Over the next few decades we may become increasingly buffeted by worldwide markets. If so, the farming in

ABOVE: Blue Grey cow.
BELOW: Pink Grey Bill Grayson.

areas like this will become less and less economically viable.

Pen-y-Ghent, looming in the distance, itself had three broad rakes of tumbled stone on its side. They were caused by a thunderstorm, in July 1881, that washed away the soil and turned the River Ribble into a rushing torrent twenty yards wide. Extreme weather is not restricted to our age. Nature will intervene. Perhaps, even on our densely populated island, we could allow it to do so more freely, and permit more unadorned, ungrazed, cheap wilderness?

I was still exploring karst country, and a little further south, at the edge of the Yorkshire Dales, I visited Malham Cove. It looks like a quarry but at one time a river, bigger than the Ribble in full spate, tumbled over its rim. Falls as big as Niagara, apparently, smoothed the top and sides of this huge white wall. The river has gone elsewhere.

The stream that runs away from Malham Cove and winds through a bottle-green valley is no rolling thunder now. Alders line its bank. Ash trees clothe the base of the cliff. Way above their feathery tops I could see a few tiny figures high on the sheer wall, and I could hear, echoing along the river, the ancient call of the wild. Greta Elkin was yodelling to me.

A native of Northern Ireland, Greta was Britain's champion yodeller. She has played the Grand Ole Opry and opened for Willie Nelson in Nashville. She was sitting on a stone at the water's edge demonstrating why the famous warble has made its way from the Matterhorn to Christina Aguilera.

Yodelling seems to hit the wavelength to set up an echo, and this is the reason that it is so associated with the Alps. Shepherds in Switzerland yodelled to one another across valleys, and still do if you slip them a fiver. Immigrants took the idea to the cattle ranches of North America and the yodel made its way into early country music.

Greta was addicted to the country sound as a girl and remembers that her first influence was Slim Whitman, who had a big hit with his 'cow call'. 'Ooooh, oooh, oooie oooo ooh ooh. Ooooh, oooh, oo oo ooh, ooh,' it went. There was a time when it was more important to stick a bit of ululation in a country song than wear a stetson. And now, in the spirit of 'She Taught Me How to Yodel', another of her early influences, and one she covers rather beautifully, Greta set to work to

refine my distinctly raw technique.

It was a doomed task. I could get the quivering going. Sometimes my falsetto fluted out like a train whistle. Sometimes my throaty wobble pulsated and, like a faulty fairground pipe organ, a yodel would break out. I frightened the rock climbers with this primeval sound, emerging from the ash spinney below them, but I never really mastered the musical possibilities.

The hills have always been associated with communication. I suppose we could have picked a spookier day to go up to Cross Fell, the highest point in the Pennines, some distance farther north in Cumbria and almost into border country. Perhaps we could have chosen a day when the clouds dripped blood or three moons came out, for, at one time, the place was known as a haunt of fiends. As it was, we had to content ourselves with a thick, looming fog caused by low cloud.

ABOVE: Karst country is formed by limestone deposits.

It was an odd experience to drive my camper van into the thick of it. Despite all the warnings, I had enjoyed glorious views from most of the summits I visited. Or I had walked up slowly and hardly noticed the way the mist had thickened around me.

To get to Cross Fell we took a side turning, unlocked a special gate and soon found ourselves driving up an unnerving private road, the sort where there aren't enough cars to stop the grass growing in little tussocks in the middle. I had no idea where we were, but we came to a thick mesh fence with another locked gate – and then the stuff of my nightmares.

It was in *Garry Halliday*, now long forgotten even by television trivia nuts, that Garry (played by Terence Longdon) and Bill Dodds (Terence Alexander) spent hours sitting at the controls of an aeroplane being menaced by 'The Voice'. To signify heightened tension, and to terrify six-year-old Griff, the director would cut to a bleak hill topped by an alien, golf-ball-like structure. Now a similar pale and mysterious object loomed out of the mist in front of me. Mundanely, it was the Great Dun Fell Radar & Radio Station, but to me it would always be a portent of just-after-high-tea doom.

Of course mountains have always had their uses. Not just for mines and water or timber, but also as lookout posts. The earliest long-distance express messages were sent by beacons on high places. It seems a little banal that our modern electrical systems are just as reliant on height, but Mark the engineer, who opened his heavy security door and showed us around, explained the obvious when I asked the obvious. The extra height of the fell added about seventy-five miles of radar capability to the installation. And they weren't there to spot UFOs. They were there to cover an enormous area of British airspace for the civilian air authorities and ensure that planes didn't bash into each other.

I was hoping the inside of the radar station would be a mass of bleeping lights and low, sinister background noise, but it was like the interior of a school cupboard. Inside Cross Fell there were a lot of firmly closed metal cabinets. The radar dish was driven by a couple of big electric motors in a room like a storage unit. This was filled with bits of scaffolding and some spare parts in boxes, and illuminated by flickering neon strip lighting. I was led through bare corridors into another big, over-lit room with a double avenue of free-standing cabinets. On a

RIGHT: Malham Cove defied my yodel.

'Well, did it get up?'

'No, it's still in the pond.'

'Oh.'

Then I saw one further away. 'Ohhhh. Look. Over there!' It was not actually in my pool, but one pool further down the ladder. A big fish had leapt straight into the crest of the fall, frantically waving its fins as if trying to get a little grip on the flood charging past, but it had fallen back in exhaustion. 'Did you get that?'

'No.'

Moving on, we came to Derbyshire. Thomas Hobbes, the philosopher who once noted that life was 'nasty, brutish and short', wrote a poem in praise of the Peak District called 'De Mirabilibus Pecci'. Later, translated from the Latin as 'The Wonders of the Peaks', it became a rather popular item, drawing attention to a miraculous well, the alpine qualities of the hills and, of course, the extraordinary and forbidding limestone caves.

A few years later Daniel Defoe, the author of *Robinson Crusoe*, passing by on his *Tour through the Whole Island of Great Britain*, decided to check out these wonders. Alas, he was not impressed, particularly with the underground candidates. He wrote that if you were the sort of person overawed by the chimney at the back of a fireplace, then you would find something to impress you in the Derbyshire caves. However, I sense that neither Hobbes nor Defoe actually went properly potholing but simply stood at the entrance with a fiery brand and a squint.

To get a real impression of the wonders of the Peaks it is necessary to venture a little way into the ground. Dave 'Moose' Nixon was on hand to guide me, and he took me to Giant's Hole.

Just off the road we came to what seemed to me a rather clichéd entrance to a cave. It was a big, black hole with broken rock all around it, rather like a grotto in an Italian garden. A dark tunnel obligingly disappeared into the side of the hill, almost inviting the passer-by to go in and poke about. It was all rather obvious. Cavemen must have thrived in Derbyshire.

The inside had the look of not very expertly carved polystyrene. We could have been in a *Doctor Who* set, except for the cold, cold, clear water gurgling past our wellies. As well as the wellies, I had a 'lid' on, which severely restricted my natural

LEFT: I miss a leaping salmon for the sixth time.

upward view and ensured that I continually bashed my head against the ceiling, incurring observations along the lines of 'Aren't you glad you wore your helmet?' But Dave was a practical Acheron, leading me into his underworld. 'We're not like climbers who are always looking for the most difficult route up anything. We get down there and get back as best we can,' he said.

Giant's Hole was a beginner's cave. It was drippy and flooded underfoot, but I was pleased to see that there was a uniform, man-sized height to it.

'Well, actually, a previous owner of the land started knocking the more difficult bits out,' Dave explained. 'He was trying to open it to the public, but they put a stop to that.'

Even so, it was easy enough to take parties of schoolchildren a few feet down to look at the chamber – easy enough to take me even.

Water has a lot to do with the cave system. Here in the White Peaks the hills are made of gritstone, shale and limestone, and the limestone allows water to seep through its cracks and natural faults. Because limestone dissolves in water, slowly the fissures become widened.

'But this isn't always a human size?' I quizzed Dave. 'I mean, isn't claustrophobia to the caveman what vertigo is to a mountain climber? Don't you get to a point where you think, I can't get through there? I'm stuck. The hole is too small.'

'Well, then we sort of reach for our pick and hack our way through.'

I was still puzzled. 'What if there's nothing beyond? How can you guarantee that there will be more passage on the other side?'

'We put dye in the water. It comes out further down and so we know that there are ways through. Dye is one of the explorer's weapons.'

As we went on, the tunnel suddenly descended. Here the rock formations were more obviously cave-like, with stalactites forming and great bulbs of organic-looking, tuberous 'candle-flow' rock on the walls.

'You could stand in this place for a hundred years,' Dave told me, putting a hand on one of them, 'and you wouldn't note any appreciable change. These things have taken thousands of thousands of years to form.'

We had to clamber up a ledge, twist and turn and at one point get down on our hands and knees. Ahead of us I could hear a gushing sound. We squeezed through and entered first a big space with a waist-high waterfall, like some decoration in an expensive Chinese restaurant, and then we came into a much grander space indeed.

There was a good deal more to Giant's Hole than the back of a fireplace. Leaning outwards, I could barely see my light reflecting on the upper levels. We were in a massive chamber. Again it was very wet. The gurgle of water and the steady, echoey dripping noise never stopped. The walls oozed, the rocks glistened with damp and it was cold. Dave assured me, though, that the temperature was fairly constant, and on a cold winter's day it was quite often warmer underground than it was up top.

Up top. Ah yes, now where was that exactly? It was a few hundred yards behind us. I got just a little frisson, just a hint of the nightmarish claustrophobia. The rocks where we were sitting were bulbed and wrinkled like giant gourds, and orange in colour too, but solid – proper stone. We put lights on in order to film, and finally revealed, way above our heads, the narrowing top; tent-like and gloomy. It was like a taking a break in a mountain king's urinal. You wouldn't want to linger. This was no home from home.

The point of caving was to move on, not to admire the view. It was still an exploratory sport, as mountaineering had been two hundred years before. Dave had recently discovered Titan. I realized that I had read about this quite recently and was actually in a position to tell him about it.

'It was an enormous cave, wasn't it?'

'You could fit the entire London Eye inside it.'

They had used dye to discover that as well. And because it had taken three weeks for the dye to re-emerge into the cave's water system they had guessed that there was something ginormous holding on to the water. They had broken through by excavating a tunnel in a lead mine, which confirmed the interconnectedness of mines and caves, but since then had sunk another shaft that brought them in at the top. We couldn't have filmed in Titan. Quite simply the largest underground chamber in Britain, it would have needed a much bigger lighting budget than we had.

Having feasted my eyes on Giant's Hole, I was eager for a bit more. The stream at my feet rushed on and into another black tunnel in the far corner.

'Can you go down there?'

'Oh yes. It goes on a lot further, it's 4.3 km long.' Dave paused. 'But it gets a little bit tricky.'

I think he meant I'd have to use some of my rock-climbing and diving skills, and I think somebody had told him they were about as developed as my horsemanship, so we decided to leave it. I had some walking to do. I was going to Kinder Scout.

'Benny Rothman was quite a short chap,' Roly Smith, author of over sixty books on walking and the countryside, told me the following morning. 'He was in his seventies, but we went on a ramble up on Kinder Scout a few years ago, just before he died, and I had difficulty keeping up.'

And Benny must have been pretty nimble in 1932 too, I thought, as I looked for a way of shinning up to the outcrop where he had stood to enthuse his band of mass trespassers before they began their assault on Kinder Scout.

I had assembled my own crowd. And I wanted to address them before we set off, but I stopped when I saw about ten or so black guys coming along the road to join us. Maxwell, Donald, Mark and the others were members of a regular walking group.

'Black men suffer a lot from silly diseases in middle age,' Max told me. 'They get late-development diabetes and heart problems, and we wanted to get some of our people out on their feet, walking … so we walk.'

It was startling and dreadful to notice how incongruous black walkers seemed. I realized that I had seen so few black people out on the hills and sort of accepted it unthinkingly.

'But that's what we believe,' Donald said. 'People think a black man out walking looks odd. So how do you think a black person feels? We have to get people to realize that they can get out there and walk and that's why we go together in a group.'

I took the easiest route up the cliff to address our own mass-trespass re-enactment. The quarry was now a decorous car park with saplings growing up around it, golden-hued in the sharp autumn and a bit spiky too. I banged my way through and clambered up the rocks as best I could; to pretend to be Benny for a bit and urge on our collection of rangers, rambling officials and black walkers.

I like the idea of Benny. The little Sheffield mechanic was filled with the righteous anger of the short and intelligent. In those days there were very few paths over the high moors. The sole route across one had only been agreed with the land owners in 1896, and the young Manchester ramblers, mostly members of the

Communist Party-inspired Workers Sports' Federation, thought it was time to reclaim the heath, the upper levels and the steep bits.

Kinder Scout rises up in a big, table-mountain crest and on its story-book ridge there is a waterfall that is famous for going the wrong way in big weather. In the wind the so-called Kinder Downfall was now an upfall, and even from several miles away we could see the great sheets of water lashing upwards. But we were so close to Manchester that a short bus ride was all it would have needed to leave this inspiriting waste of emptiness and get back to town.

As we walked up, a quick look at the peaty vastness stretching away, bleak and pointless, was enough to make me see that anyone would rail at the idea that this was private. If your country garden is the size of a county it should be able to take the imprint of what, after all, is only the venturesome.

Privately, even back then, individuals rambled about at will, but they went

ABOVE: Our memorial mass ramble spots the café.

walking in neurotic fear of the gamekeepers, who became stroppy if encountered. This I understood. Walking about the countryside can still be a stressful experience. Who wants to cross a farmyard, even if it is on a footpath, and risk some red-faced lout rushing out and shouting at you? We don't like it. Legitimacy is vital.

In the 1930s a group of ramblers met some gamekeepers on Kinder Scout and were ordered off the land. 'The owners' ancestors fought battles to gain this land,' a keeper said. One rambler took off his coat and offered to fight to get it back. But on the day of the original protest ramble, it wasn't the trespass itself that caused the trouble. Nor did the ramblers venture far on to the moors. After less than two miles they left the footpath and immediately confronted the gamekeepers, who had been anticipating this well-advertised intrusion and were lying in wait.

Today I was surprised by how quickly we covered their route. We barely set foot

on the moors. Turning around, we could easily look down, over another reservoir, towards the woods from where we had set off.

In 1932 things did not go according to plan. Because the ramblers were many and the keepers few, for once the walkers had the upper hand. There was a struggle (or rather a bit of pushing and shoving). One of the keepers slipped and fell, knocking himself unconscious on a stone. The ramblers gallantly went to his aid.

Shortly afterwards they were joined by the Sheffield groups who had come most of the way unopposed, from the other direction. They all went down again together to Manchester. But, as they came off the moors, the police were waiting, and arrested those they saw as the ringleaders. To most people's astonishment, these men were given jail sentences. It was this that served to radicalize the ramblers' cause. The British legal system appeared to protect the right of a few to sequester an immense area of open, bare moorland that the few rarely visited, simply to prevent others from setting foot on it, but it took another seventy years for the 'right to roam' to reach the statute books.

They had held an anniversary celebration a few years ago. 'The Duke of Devonshire was keen to apologize. He had sent messages and then asked if he could come. In a way his speech was the most moving. He apologized for the actions of his grandfather. And the big estates now largely believe that grouse and walkers can coexist,' Roly told me.

Ironically, today it is the park rangers who ask people to keep to the footpaths, but it's because of the danger of erosion, not to protect the rights of the few.

Our memorial ramble stood together for a moment, looking back the way we had come. It was a blowy, grey-streaked day. It was just the sort of day, in fact, when almost anybody would look out of the window and say 'forget it'. It was the sort of day you might think twice about even going out to the shops. The rain was slewing across the umber ridge. Big clouds were sailing by at hat height. But we had passed dozens of walkers making their way across these moors on a weekend jolly. They all knew that the weather, however bad, was not so much a hindrance as part of the experience itself.

It was, as Max said, turning to me with a smile, 'bloody marvellous'.

LEFT: An exemplary silly hat.

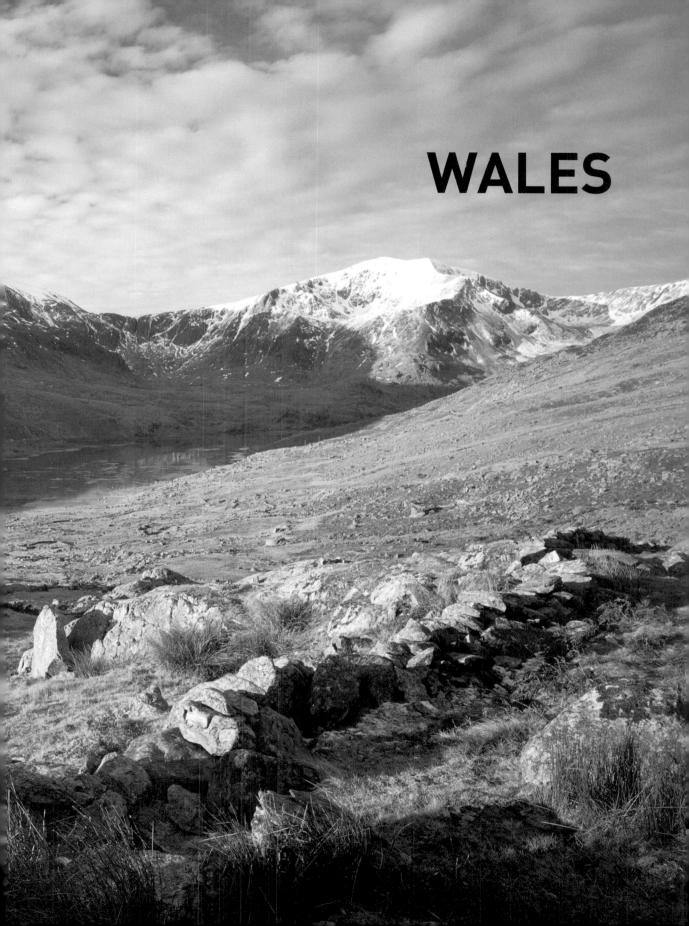

WALES

CHAPTER FIVE

Wales

When I first waded up Ben Hope, on that initial outing, through thigh-high snow, with those frozen-pea balls of ice rattling against my anorak, I started madly fantasizing about the summer. I like snow. I associate it with snowmen and days off school, but I imagined the glorious mountain days to come.

Soon I would be a happy goatherd on a sunny alp, I would scamper under blazing August suns in unbecoming shorts. I would turn a nutty brown and sing half-remembered yodelling songs to Paul, my six-foot-six assistant.

I think it was about six months later that I began to think, hmm, it has rained, it has been cold, it has nearly blown me off several cliffs, but it has not yet allowed me to wear one of my short-sleeved climbing shirts in purple, loose-weave knit, has it? In fact, wait a minute, it has become winter again, hasn't it? What happened to the summer? And now I was going to North Wales, where the annual rainfall was measured in kilometres. It was going to be horrible all over again before it ever got nice.

Fortunately, my director, Ross, had made a pact with the devil. Not only did the sun shine, it shone at an acute, equinoctial angle. God became a Hollywood lighting director. The folds and inclines of Eryri ('the Haunt of the Eagles') were illuminated by a low, slanting glow made of sharp outlines and crisp vistas in a slightly cold air for the entire time we were in Wales.

On that first early morning we walked up 700 metres and the stones were already covered with a smattering of frost. The long, triangular slope opposite was topped with a silver dust. It was a change of season. The sky was still blue but the long lines

RIGHT: Eryri – the Haunt of Eagles.

of cumulus, flattened underneath like scones on a tray, were pink and gold-grey tinged, with rain at the centre. Our breath showed.

Sitting on Elidir Fawr I could look over a beginner's relief map of the western British Isles. Every climb was to become worth it for the view, but on that first day the whole place beckoned.

To the right, I could clearly see the Isle of Man. Turning slightly, there was the flat plain of Anglesey and beyond that, incredibly, quite a lot of Ireland. Just a little to the left was a mass of mountain peaks, the Lleyn peninsula. ('That was where they had burnt the Englishman's cottages,' Alan George, my guide, told me later.) It was Welsh Wales, where the language was strongest and the hills hilliest. Turning further to the south, the mountains romped away in perfect, clean detail towards the second-highest peak in Wales, Cadair Idris, about forty miles away. But dominating everything was the crowned ridge in front of me –Yr Wyddfa:

Snowdon itself, the highest mountain in Wales, which, unlike Ben Nevis, didn't appear as a big, inverted cone but more as a huge, warm creature's back sleeping in the morning light.

This is the sort of place that encourages speculative, metaphoric myths. On the other side, behind my back, in the valleys of the River Conwy, the country is like Bohemia, with little wooded hillocks and quaint fortified houses protecting crooked bridges. Up here I could trace the wakes of ancient ships from Ireland. I was looking down on the Menai Strait, across which Roman legionaries had launched an attack on the druids. I could imagine the trouble that successive generations of English kings had experienced in penetrating these mountains and see exactly why independent medieval Welsh kingdoms, run by lots of Griffiths, had flourished here. Just by looking around, and by allowing the geography to tell its history, I was becoming dangerously, romantically Welsh.

I am a bogus Griffith. I get stick from the deeply real Welsh. *The Guardian* ran an article accusing me of being a 'disingenuous' Welshman. (I would never be forgiven some weak jokes made in 1978, apparently.) And, yes, I dislike all that bard, harp and 'subject nation' stuff. But even I could see why this was a country that engendered fairy stories.

There are thousands of legends about the monsters, dragons and warriors of this region. Cadair Idris means 'the throne of Idris'. But it was a giant, Rhita, who lived on it. He was known as 'the beard collector'. He wore a cloak woven from the whiskers of the men he had butchered. A rival giant lived on Snowdon. They had an argument, as big men tend to, which resulted in them tearing up chunks of the land and throwing it at each other.

This myth tried to explain the landscape, and probably warned children not to wander too far up the mountain as well. Wandering myself, I soon encountered the sort of scenery that seems to require explanation. The valley of Llanberis is littered with colossal boulders, independent lumps of rock, just sitting there – so huge that they have to build roads around them. What Ruskin described as the essential quality of mountains, their decrepitude, their sheer state of collapse, literally stops you in your tracks.

Today Snowdon, approached from these low roads, quickly reveals that it is the closest remote mountain to the great cities of Birmingham, Liverpool and

LEFT: Sitting on Elidir Fawr contemplating speculative, metaphoric myths.

Manchester. Eight and half million visitors come every year. Strolling down into Llanberis to get up to the summit, I was mobbed by a posse of old ladies from Gloucestershire. They were on their way up to the top too, in their cardies and going-to-church hats. No need for Gore-tex breathable outer shells here. We were taking the train.

The Snowdon Mountain Railway runs on a Swiss rack-and-pinion system. Operating for over 100 years, it still uses the original locomotives, and, as I boarded, these puffed self-important jets of steam in the station; before trundling upwards at a cautious, stately pace – rather befitting the old-age pensioners, the ancient carriages and myself.

It felt quite different from an Alpine funicular, at least it did once we had made the initial lurch through a bit of forest and past a waterfall, straight out of the station. Instead of the precipitous, rocky, pine-clad channel of a ski-lift, the railway pops out on to a bare, sweeping landscape, utterly uneventful in the foreground, but broad and compelling in the long view. The mountain became like a series of vast, shifting screens. Down at the bottom I spotted a tiny, isolated farmhouse, but otherwise the place looked as if it had been cleared for a mythical giant's round of golf.

We got only halfway up because there were engineering works on the line. This was more like being on Connex than I had thought. We all disembarked at a featureless platform high up in the middle of nowhere in particular. The old biddies wandered about like chickens, nervously walking a little way towards a sheer cliff overlooking Cwm Hetiau, or 'the Valley of the Hats'. (It was given this name because the locals far below had for a while made a living collecting the hats blown down there from the open carriages.) But for the most part our party stayed near their mobile hutch and looked a little disconcerted by so much space all around them. Not for long. The engine gave a toot and within minutes they were back aboard and the carriages were snaking off down the mountain. The train, which could carry so many up so quickly, became no more than a miniature toy on the flank of Yr Wyddfa.

It was pretty, but it was noticeable. When the flanks of a high place are quite so naked they can hardly absorb any intrusion. Even the paths make their mark. They

ABOVE: Safe on a Swiss rack-and-pinion system – unless you jump out of the window.

criss and cross the mountains, like scratches on the side of a car.

Visitors have to follow a route. They don't want to get lost. But they gradually wear the surface down to mud. Naturally they prefer not to walk in the mud, so they step to one side and spread the mud, until a great motorway of mud scars up the side of the hill. The National Trust or the Snowdonia park authorities build paths to accommodate them. Close to, these are marvels of construction – Appian Ways to the skies; great chunks of rock, manoeuvred to make a steady progression of steps up the mountain. They are perfectly organic – solid, dependable (except in the winter, when the surface gets covered with invisible skeins of ice), buttressed and lovingly constructed, especially where they bridge the rivulets with slabs, or part the way with channels, to allow the constant, oozing-sponge sides of the mountain to weep into the valley.

Tramping upwards, path and railway track went side by side and I decided that

ABOVE: A huge warm creature's back, sleeping in the morning light – Snowdon and its visible paths.

the railway track was not much more intrusive than the walking track. It gave me a chance to look a bit more closely at the rack-and-pinion system too. I sat down to examine it.

There has only ever been a single accident on the Snowdon Mountain Railway. Worryingly, it happened on the opening day, Easter Monday 1896, when one of the engines broke free and hurtled off the mountain. Two climbers below looked up to see a steam locomotive falling out of the clouds. The passengers would have been startled but safe, except that one of them was hanging out of the window. He saw the driver and fireman leap out, and decided to do the same. He hit his head on the rocks and died, while the carriages came to a halt under their own braking system. (A second train later crashed into them, as the communications cable had been cut by the runaway locomotive.)

This doesn't seem to have discouraged visitors much. The pinnacle was the noisiest mountain I had ever visited. The weather was warm. The sky was blue. There wasn't much of a wind. It was the middle of an ordinary weekday in September. It was like visiting some popular, seaside belvedere lookout. I half expected ice-cream sellers and pigeons. And the racket! The old café (to His Royal Highness the Prince of Wales 'the highest slum in the land') was being jack-hammered to bits so they could build the highest award-winning architectural carbuncle in the land. One of the builders' trains was rattling into the station. Below our feet a training jet was screaming home, while a yellow Royal Air Force Mountain Rescue helicopter yammered busily up the other side of the mountain.

I got into a queue waiting to clamber on to the concrete roundel marking the highest spot. When it was, at last, my turn, I enjoyed a few moments gazing out at the brilliant, 180-degree vision of lonelier, quieter peaks.

Nearly everybody who climbs mountains somehow resents anyone else doing the same. Still, I suppose I could have come on a bank holiday. But on a little stroll around the summit, I started to notice the plastic bottles shoved into crevices, the banana skins, the sweet wrappers, the plastic and the cigarette butts. We were miles from public services. There wasn't actually a rubbish bin. (That would be absurd, wouldn't it – to climb a mountain and find a bin at the top? It would feel like a satirical cartoon.) But someone left this stuff. This was our collective, non-carbon footprint.

I was probably noticing it more than usual, because I was meeting up with a bloke called Rob the Rubbish. Robin Kevan had been a social worker and on retirement had decided to clean mountains as a hobby. He had in fact already led an expedition to clean up the peak I was examining so minutely.

Rob proved to be an unnervingly delightful chap. He disliked litter so he had put on a day-glo jacket, taken up his claw-stick and, like some medieval holy man, dedicated his life to wandering the wild places on behalf of us sinners. And he had a jacket for me too. It said, 'Griff the Garbage'.

'Is this to stop us being run down by a passing lorry, then?'

'It sort of gives me a bogus official status,' Rob laughed. 'Sometimes people come over and actually give me stuff to take down for them.'

He had started in his own backyard, in Llanwrtyd Wells, getting up at dawn '…because the council never seemed to clean the verges round our place, and it sort of grew from there.'

I worried on his behalf that this could grow into a horrible obsession. We are a dirty people. Every part of our country is littered with some sort of rubbish. Llanwrtyd Wells is known as 'the smallest town in Britain'. What if Rob found he couldn't stop – like some crazed housewife – hoovering Powys, then Britain, then the world? Already somebody was taking him to Everest, where the climbers' trash includes, as well as oxygen bottles and used equipment, a few dead bodies.

At least on Everest fear and exhaustion can be used as excuses. And I suppose I could understand the very pinnacle of Snowdon being trashed too. All paths lead to the peak. There's no room at the top. But I suspected that our little experiment, halfway down the mountain, some way off the path (to make use of an attractive background) would need to be faked for the camera. I was wrong.

We took black plastic bags and I struck pay dirt straight away. It was quite exciting. 'Rob! Rob! A tissue,' I cried. But Rob was already busy, scooping up a couple of tins and some sort of hairnet. He has led two expeditions now up the main path of Ben Nevis. He has done the Cheviots and Pen-y-Fan in the Brecon Beacons, as well as Snowdon. I walked on. Ahead of me, placed quite carefully to one side of a stone, were two full plastic bottles of water.

Rob emptied them smilingly. 'They must have brought them up, quite sensibly, and then got tired of carrying them.' He threw them in his bag. On we

RIGHT: A busy day on the summit. Plenty of room on top.

went. In half an hour our bags were half full. I was reminded of the myth of Sisyphus, doomed to endlessly push his boulder up a mountain only to have it roll back down again.

There was another human intrusion into the landscape that I had been alerted to. I nearly trod in it.

The very top of this most famous of Welsh mountains has an exquisite, stepped, pyramidal shape. It is not a bare, bald, stony cap, but, especially to the south, a descending series of steep, grassy levels. I was going down, needing both hands to steady myself, when I noticed at eye level what appeared to be two dark-red tropical flowers. They were peeking round a shale outcrop. I was puzzled. I leant in. They seemed to be made of cloth; not plastic exactly, but the more expensive silk-and-taffeta hybrid, with green wired stems. They had been poked into the earth by the side of … and I started back, guiltily, because they had been lain next to a carefully strewn little bed of white ash. These were human remains.

An increasing number of people when they die want their ashes to be scattered on Snowdon. I can understand the sentiment. The mountain top has a noble, spiritual mien. Perhaps grandfather was a mountain walker. Perhaps a nationalist. Perhaps he always meant to come here himself but never quite managed it.

I confess my own dad is currently somewhere on his favourite mud bank in a Suffolk river where he sailed his boat.

This little grave had been quite carefully hidden. I felt horribly intrusive. But if I was intrusive, what were they? One park ranger has described it as, some mornings, resembling a dusting of frost. Professor Des Thompson, an uplands adviser, has pointed out that the ash is also adding to the fertility of what really ought to be naturally poor soil. The dead are literally pushing up daisies. Some people are leaving little plaques or crosses, or other, non-organic memorials. It grieves me to point this out, but the red silk flowers were not going to break down and mulch the upper ground. They would eventually blow away and presumably provide more work for Rob the Rubbish.

Despite the railways and the café and the funerals, Snowdon is still a dangerous place. Twelve to fourteen people die in these hills every year. This is quite a toll, in this health-and-safety-conscious age. Nobody signs a certificate, takes a test, passes a medical or crosses a barrier before they take a hike in the peaks. When I met up with the Llanberis Mountain Rescue Team for a training exercise, this was the element that intrigued me

They are the busiest team in Britain. They have sixty-two members, all volunteers, and ten or so were out this afternoon on a training exercise, partly to test a new self-assembly, lightweight stretcher, which they liked a great deal (though they told me they will love the model that they're actually going to get – a titanium one – even more).

They were all a little tired because they had been out the night before, in appalling rain, transporting a real sixteen-and-a-half-stone man with a broken ankle down off the highest part of the ridge opposite us.

It had been a standard evening out for them. There had already been eighty-nine incidents in 2006, including searches ('We asked one couple when was the last time they knew exactly where they were and they said when they were on the M56'). This team had faced a range of broken ankles, feet and backs, from falls, and two fatalities. And they always went out, whatever the circumstances.

Now I was going to play the victim. They wanted me to get into their new stretcher. They laid me down in a sort of shiny aluminium cage, and started

LEFT: Going down is when accidents happen.

strapping me up like a papoose. The stretcher was collapsible, but luckily only at their behest.

'Tighter!'

I had webbing around my chest, stomach and legs. They heaved it tighter. I could still just about talk. So I did.

'But what happens with your jobs and things?'

'You have to have an understanding boss.' Louise worked for an outdoor-wear company. 'Sometimes, though, you know, nice day and a boring presentation to do...'

Daffyd taught in a special-needs school. Gwyn sold safety equipment. Cathy was a hairdresser – 'I had to leave one woman, half her hair was done, on one side only.' But it was the late evening calls that buggered you up. Sometimes it wasn't so bad, when it was your turn to put the kids to bed, 'but after you'd already put yourself to bed, to get up and out, whew! Who really understands?'

Who indeed? It takes four hours to get to the top of a Welsh mountain. Another four to get down. In daylight, carrying a stretcher over difficult slopes, it needs a team of ten. They try to ask casualties to walk if they possibly can. And they like it when the helicopter arrives.

They picked me up, fixed ropes to the harnesses and lowered me over the edge. I couldn't move anything except my head, and that only a few inches. First, sky, then a slight lurch and a view of the ridge opposite, and then scrapes and bumps.

Louise abseiled down in front of me, smiling and chatting – to reassure me, I suppose – except that it was a lovely day and this was just training, and it was the most comfortable, effortless descent of a mountain I had so far made. Mind you, I wasn't suffering from a heart attack, frightened, cold or exhausted. Louise kept asking me if I was all right. Frankly, I found it incredibly soothing. 'Ha, ha,' I chortled. 'I can imagine people paying a lot of money for this sort of thing in a basement in King's Cross.'

I wished I hadn't said that, actually. Louise was an attractive woman. Her husband was on the team too. I was tied to a rack.

They lifted me up and carried me gingerly along a path.

'Don't you ever feel ... resentful towards the people who have got you out of bed?'

RIGHT: Is it too late for second thoughts about being lifted by helicopter?

'Oh no.'

But I wanted to pursue this. 'So what proportion of call-outs are false alarms?'

'Very few. They did once prosecute some drunks at a party in Manchester who had been pretending that they were lost on a mountain.'

'I meant people who go out unprepared and get lost or stranded through their own foolishness.'

'Oh, I see.' This needed a bit more consideration. 'No, no, less than ten per cent. Accidents happen. Sometimes people underestimate how fit you need to be, but to get that far away you need a bit of commitment in the first place.'

I had heard the same from other Mountain Rescue teams. They knew they were needed for genuine accidents and were prepared to take the occasional stupidity as part of the price. But I still thought someone should invent a rubberized pogo stick protruding from the bottom of the stretcher so the team could bounce their casualties down the mountain.

For the time being their principal concern was to get the stretcher to a reasonable piece of flat land, where a helicopter could come in. And then a mighty racket started, just a little way out of my vision. What followed should have been a thrilling, terrifying experience, but I was an embedded observer. 'Never sit when you can stand, never stand when you can lie,' Winston Churchill once advised. 'Never lie when you can be tied up securely in a thunderous cacophony and watch several hundred tons of square yellow metal finally slide into place above you,' I say. Two balls stuck out the side. Oh, those are men in helmets, I remember thinking, and then a little creature with a big head suddenly started getting bigger. It was an aircrew man being lowered down to me on a winch.

He was brisk and efficient. 'Hi,' he said. 'It can get warm by the engine exhausts, but it's nothing to worry about.' There was a lurch and this time the big yellow object started getting bigger. Within seconds I was right up underneath a truncated wing and then, with another lurch, clearly inside, and looking up at the ceiling of a Sea King helicopter.

A minute later I sat on a little bench wearing an enormous metal football myself. ('Pull the whole thing by the straps otherwise you'll catch your ears.') The noise was momentarily deadened. A dangling lead was plugged into the frame above my head and I could hear the pilot on a fuzzy radio saying, 'Hello.' If I

RIGHT: The most comfortable, effortless descent of a mountain I had so far made.

looked forward, past the ribs of the utterly utilitarian, truck-like interior, I could see an arm waving from in front of the windscreen. That was him. I crawled across a mud-green rubber mat, washable for the blood, and perched next to Flight Lieutenant Lindsey Smith, a slight, pretty girl and a spare pilot, while the sides of Eryri slid past outside the windows, and little model people walking on the mountain waved at us from the crest. We were already on our way back to base in Anglesey.

Lindsey explained that real accidents usually happened in difficult terrain. The pilots had to make complicated judgements about fog, or low cloud in storms at night. Her own most exciting rescue had been of some children who were stuck on a sandbank with a rising tide, impossible to find in low cloud, until a sudden break provided a fleeting glimpse and allowed her to get down.

'What,' I asked her, 'has all this to do with the defence of the realm?'

'It's the best training. In real conditions. It's part of our job.'

In fact the Mountain Rescue Service was originally developed by the RAF here on Anglesey. The base had been a vital part of operations in the Second World War, first as Sector Operations Centre for the control of fighter defences in the approaches to Merseyside and Belfast, and the protection of shipping in the Irish Sea, and then as a first stopping point for planes from the United States, but the approaches across the mountains proved fatal. The science of wind channelling was in its infancy. They were losing planes at the rate of six a week. Any crew which survived the crashes could die from exposure on the mountainside before help came. That was because there was no help. It took the efforts of one officer fighting an indifferent service bureaucracy to finally get a few surplus wellington boots and an old ambulance.

Today we were setting down in a massive yellow helicopter, one of three operating round the clock. We landed on a tarmac island in front of some forties huts, on a massive base, waiting for the rotors to stop, because they hang down low on an aircraft like this, and walking across to an interior which felt like a school with purpose. Alongside adverts for theatres and keep-fit classes were team photographs of courtesy visits and inspections, aeroplane memorabilia, mounted squadron crests and wall charts familiarizing the casual reader with missile developments and the Suez War. Everywhere there were maps of enormous scale. We didn't get time to pose for a photograph. The crew removed their helmets and put them straight back on. A small boy had broken an ankle out on an island off the Lleyn peninsula. They walked back out of the door and took off in less than a minute.

The following day Barbara Jones and I climbed up to get to the 'lake where no birds fly'. And no birds did fly over the dark waters filling the basin of the 'murderous place', as Thomas Pennant, an earlier traveller, named it with a palpable shudder. He was probably referring to the legend of Idwal, the clever son of Prince Owain of Gwynedd, who was drowned in Llyn Idwal by an oafish uncle, jealous of his nephew's abilities, and, then, was too stupid to lie convincingly about what he had done. Owain named the lake Idwal in memory of his son. Folklore has it that no bird flies over the lake's surface and that a wailing voice can be heard when there is a storm in the Cwm. It was a parable of the early Middle Ages. ('Don't be a clever wain with us, boyo.')

LEFT: Several hundred tons of square yellow metal slides into place.

We were there to look for alpine plants. Barbara was a botanist and she was taking me up in the footsteps, or the handholds, of the earliest rock climbers. Some say this was Coleridge, others claim the crown for the Reverend William Green and his companion Reverend William Bingley, who, slithering about these grey faces of granite, were said to be the first to rope themselves up and lower themselves down the sheer sides of a mountain.

In truth, there were probably hundreds of anonymous gull egg collectors or crystal pickers or sheep rescuers who had hung off the cliffs long before these two intrepid botanists. They just failed to write about their adventures. These two did because they were searching for rare plants. It is yet another indication of how the scientists were the first to genuinely explore some of these remote places, but it is also a measure of how damp and cold and icy this particular bit of Wales can be. It is one of the few places where arctic-alpine wild flowers grow in Britain.

Barbara soon had me scurrying around the rocks myself. We were looking for a particular rare type of lily, the Snowdon lily, but I started to notice that there was an extraordinary variety of miniature rockery plants poking up in the damp hollows. I say rockery because the first things I discovered were little succulents, similar to the fleshy, alien, blobby plants that grew in my grandmother's garden in Weston-super-Mare: faded green in colour and cushion-leaved.

'They're lime-loving,' Barbara explained, and handed me her magnifying glass. 'Look closely at the tips of the leaves.'

Each tip came to a folded, plump v.

'Do you see the encrustation?'

There were grey crusts at the very edges. This was the plant exuding the lime it had drunk in from the rock.

We moved on and she handed me a bunch of leaves – like miniature geranium plants. 'Chew that. They call it mountain sorrel,' Barbara said. 'They used to put it into their sandwiches for a bit of flavour.' It had a sort of juicy relish, like mustard and cress. Now I was taking the magnifier from her and looking at other plants. When I concentrated they appeared to be spreading over every section of the hill. We hardly needed to rope ourselves up at all.

In fact, it wasn't the shepherds eating the plants that was the problem, it was their charges, the sheep. Just as among the limestone pavements in Yorkshire or

Tony's flock of Herdwicks in the Lake District, sheep were the dominant herbivore here, outnumbering humans in Wales by three to one. I had got used to the idea that the third of our nation that was mountainous was closely mowed and tended by the four-legged lawnmower, the white maggot, the ubiquitous baa-lamb that woke up every morning and said, 'Mmm, grass, can't wait'; that chomped and chomped and chomped at every growing thing, and determined, whether we wanted it to or not, the whole close-shaven, skinhead appearance of the British mountain. I had encountered their blank gaze on the highest tops. I had sent them lolloping dangerously off on to the most precipitous ledges to escape me.

I knew that sheep currently made little economic sense, that their coarse wool was useless except for carpets, that some believed we were overstocked and the local

ABOVE: Barbara Jones keeps a beady eye on the rare edible sorrel.

agriculture had become too dependent on them. So I was intrigued to hear that Cwm Idwal was the site of an experiment to see what would happen if sheep were banished. An area had been fenced off and left to itself. Now Barbara was going to show me it. We tramped back down the track towards the black lake, and as we walked along the track she gestured to a field on the left. 'That's it,' she said.

'That's it!'

'Yes. You can see how the birches and rowans have already got hold and the undergrowth is re-establishing itself.'

Barbara was right. There were a few young trees and quite a lot of scrub, but the area we were looking at was little more than a large garden. I had been expecting 'a swathe' at the least, or perhaps 'an expanse', but this was not much more than a couple of acres at the most. Nonetheless, as a botanist she was excited by the number of species that had established themselves. I just looked beyond at the vast plains of close-cropped mountainsides that stretched away to the hills and the bare horizon miles beyond and wondered whether we would ever allow a proportion of our wilderness to becomes just that – wilderness.

Looking back, as we walked away down the valley, Cwm Idwal played on the hairs on the back of my neck. The flat, black lake, the dripping curtains of dark cliffs, the 'smoke' vapours blowing up through a cleft in the rock known as 'the Devil's Kitchen', even a poor, soggy drowned sheep, now drifting and rolling in the wavelets on the beach, while violent squalls attacked the water and blew sudden fountains of spray high into the air – all had given the place an aura of gloomy mystery. No wonder weird stories had been invented to explain the powerful hold of the place.

Science had come to offer rational explanations. For me, though, the ones the boffins had delivered were far more mentally disconcerting than any spooky legends. These rocks were now known to be thousands of millions of years old. They were thrust up by movements of the earth's crust, floating about on its molten-metal core. The hill I was walking down was made of the debris of the debris of other mountains piled on mountains that had been formed on the other side of the planet and had crept here over millions and millions of years. The study of mountains had played a significant part in explaining the nature of the universe itself – the boiling masses of the stars, the creation of elements, the forces

ABOVE: Pondering the omnivorous sheep with a shaven mountain in the background.

of gravity … stop! This is far more frightening than any legend about giants throwing rocks about. And what is really spine-tingling is that this is all still continuing.

The mountains encouraged me to brood on metaphysics. I started pondering these huge upheavals that created them. Next I'm thinking about the age of the universe, the nature of the stars and a nice cup of coffee. Well, that's how it goes on the long walk back to the car park.

On a sunny morning in September I went to a farm on the northern edges of Eryri. We had to take a big loop around the edge of the mountains, spouting our own carbon dioxide into the clean, bright, early-autumn air, joining the motorway link that hugged the shore from Liverpool to the isle of Anglesey and came off to rise into the foothills that overlooked a startling blue sea to the west of Conwy. I had come to take part in a ritual that had its origins thousands of years

ago. We were going to round up the wild horses of North Wales.

Fferm Tyn Llwyfan lay just above the village of Llanfairfechan. As I walked up, a parliament of fowls, geese, ducks and pigeons, huddling under an oak tree, started honking and quacking. About twenty sheepdogs in a neatly constructed long pen of individual cages began yapping. Sixteen or so red-faced farmers, their sons, their uncles and their cousins, in a variety of woolly hats and mounted on a fearsome armada of fat-tyred, mud-spattered quad bikes began revving their two-stroke engines in chorus. It was the Wild Welsh Bunch. The noise was incredible. The bikes were battered and grungy. They had roared up from all the nearby farms to join in.

It was, all agreed, a lovely day for it. Everybody was making jokes in Welsh. I had been on TV the night before in a programme about a Welsh farm in Pembrokeshire so they were prepared to speak English to me. Rhys shook my hand. 'Griff, don't you hate it when they call you Reece?'

I called myself Reece. I was one of the Epping Welsh. We didn't know any better.

'It's Rrrriss, that's proper.' I thought I'd insist on that from now on. 'Hop on, Rrrriss,' shouted Gareth Wyn Jones, and without really thinking about it I sat on the back of the quad, for the most challenging part of my entire mountain journey.

The first bit was easy enough. We simply swung around a country lane at 200 miles an hour. The second stage began when we came to a gate and vaulted the first hump straight into the field. We landed with a crash that sent a judder through my entire frame, and then careered on up the hillside. I hardly had time to register the exquisite open, swelling, unfenced hills, the blue sea stretching away to the Isle of Man, the fluffy clouds suspended in the azure sky, before they disappeared in a judder of shaking vertical hold as we banged over tussock, thumped into a rut, jiggled over rough grass, skittered across a marsh and bonked, shook and crashed our way up the hill at the speed of a rocket car. I didn't know whether my fingers were going to be shaken free of their grip on the luggage rack before my arms were dragged out of their sockets or after my coccyx imploded.

And Gareth was talking all the time, casually if loudly, about what the others were doing. How they would spread out to the far gullies of this huge spread, how he was going to get me up to a handy knoll and how I was perfectly safe, even if we

LEFT: Mountains encouraging metaphysical conjecture.

were now leaning precariously over to one side and my arse was gradually slipping over the edge of the bike and my weeny fingers were loosening their hold. My eyes were drawn to a series of little drawings beneath the ignition key, now a shaking blur, of a passenger with a line through it. And then he stopped.

'Here we are, Rrriss.'

I willed my claw-like fingers to ungrip, and levered an aching limb up and over until I was quivering on the grass.

'Back in a mo.'

Gareth put his foot down. At last, now he didn't have the worry of a novice passenger, he didn't have to crawl about. He spat off over the hill in a streaking roar and left me standing alone. It was silent, but after a few moments I caught the whine of other two-stroke engines somewhere off behind a ridge. They faded. I felt like a reporter at some battle. The plain was laid out before me. I could see for miles in either direction. It was still a bright, clear, lovely day. The grass glowed a washed yellowy green. The whining buzz came momentarily on the wind. I could see the sun glinting on an impossibly miniature bike way over to the east as it bounced over a hill, and then silence again. Somewhere out there beyond my line of vision all the local farmers were scouting out their own patch of hill. There were 1000 acres of open grassland up here. They were only attending to a small part of it today and I stood waiting aimlessly, swivelling on the soles of my feet, wondering from which direction the attack would come. It was hugely exciting.

And then I saw a horse. Or rather two horses. One tubby little thing with a long, bright mane and tail nearly dragging on the floor, and an even tinier foal trotting right up close to her round tummy. They were stepping purposefully down the valley about 200 yards below me, with straight-legged determination, like a mother urging her child to hurry or they'd miss the bus. I heard a sudden roar behind me. It must be Gareth again. He soared down the semi-vertical cliff high above me and then dipped out of sight and, magically, six or seven other little dishevelled horses rose up right ahead of me, galloping together in a terrible hurry, neighing and tossing their heads, and darted off when they saw me, to rush on down and out of sight below.

Suddenly they were everywhere. Still miles away, for the most part, and seemingly running in all directions at once, single horses or pairs peeling off and

ABOVE: Wild horses wouldn't get me back on one of those quads.

exploring possible escape routes, the air beginning to fill with a constant mosquito buzzing, and little glimpses of the quad cowboys wheeling round at the top of the hills and zipping back the way they had come, to rustle in the stragglers.

Gareth roared up towards me and shot to a stop.

'There's a couple over there!' I was shouting like a crazed hunt follower, and then felt ashamed of giving them away.

'They're closing them in. We seem to be getting most of them. We're going to get them right down on that ridge over there.' Gareth pointed to where the other side of the bowl climbed to a shelf. 'Then we'll bring them down. But I'll take you to the wall now.' And I scrambled back aboard to be jolted out of my wits, on a breakneck rush down to the edge of the contained farmland, way away from the action. As we rollicked along we would startle little knots of horses hiding in the hollows and they would charge away, scattering across the valley, seemingly heading in random directions but now with their options increasingly diminishing, as their buzzing tormenters zoomed up in front of them. No, there was no escape, even though they circled towards what seemed an empty slope on the far side. I knew that at least four other bikes were lurking up behind there, like Rommel's tanks ready to cut them off where they least expected it.

Gareth abandoned me. I clambered up on to a drystone wall, not the easiest climb, looking for a foothold in a precarious heap of stones, but I was ready for the denouement now, overlooking the gap they were planning to drive them through, swaying slightly on a lichen-covered grey boulder which kept threatening to rock off the top of the wall. The distant coughing revving of the bikes rose to a whine followed by, yes, the thunder of hooves, and about thirty or forty of the ponies galloped down the hill and past me. I jumped down and ran across to where they had been finally gathered, in a triangle of walls by a gate to the road. The sun had fallen now and was shining through their manes and long tails. Their way back up the mountains was cut off by a phalanx of quads.

'They don't like to come down,' Gareth said, though they looked peaceable if wary. They would be checked for health reasons and some of the male colts taken and sold. The market for them has grown a little in recent years because it has been decided that some other heathlands would benefit from their selective grazing, so the National Trust has bought a few. And each one is separately 'owned' by one of

the farmers who had taken part in the round-up. Standing by, getting their horsey breath, I could see how small they were. These ponies had an ancient pedigree, bred out of a strain introduced by the Romans. They had survived a cull ordered by Henry VIII of all horses under twelve hands in order to provide proper, big steeds for armed men. Even then the hills had proved a refuge.

Finally the gates were opened and the junctions blocked and they trotted down the lane en masse, to the farm and a waiting, fenced field, where they tended to stick together, dignified and disdainful, anticipating the moment, a few days away, when they would be released back on to the mountain again. As for me, I was still reeling from having watched something which, despite the racket of the quad bikes, felt like a secret ancient ritual. Despite the tourists, Snowdon still had some secrets.

ABOVE: The horses coralled – dignified and disdainful and in need of a haircut.

ABOVE: With Johnny Dawes. Same shoes, different abilities.

Later I went to meet Johnny Dawes, the greatest climber of his generation, at the old Dinorwig Quarry workings. He started climbing at the age of fourteen, when he was known as 'the leaping boy'. In 1986 he had made a new route, Indian Face, on the Welsh crag Clogwyn d'ur Arddu and was credited with bringing adventure back to a sport which many felt was becoming too safe in the 1980s.

We sat on a big, flat slab of slate in the sun to put on our little climbing shoes. It was like sitting at the bottom of an empty dock. We were surrounded on three sides by sheer slate walls, cut straight out of the side of the mountain.

'Climbing is a business these days,' he explained. 'After I became famous there was a lot of interest from some of the big companies, but I wanted to concentrate on the climbs themselves. I was lucky because, in the early days, for one reason or another, I didn't really need the money associated with that sort of deal, but I got angry that others would lay claim to some of the really difficult routes just in order to pick up sponsorship.' He had found that a certain brand of climbing wear was calling itself something rather too similar to his well-known nickname – 'the stone monkey'. He felt, quite fervently, that he was 'the stone monkey', not some hat. We walked over to the wall so that he could show me what he meant.

Johnny had originally started climbing at school, not on a mountainside, but on a railway viaduct, and realized that he had something special to offer. Rock climbs are graded. We were looking at an Extremely Severe nine. They had got as far as seven before Johnny arrived and they had to start inventing extra grades, E8 and E9, for his particular skills.

He led me to a polished slab. It was a glassy wall. No natural mountain could have ended as smooth as this. Leaning right into the slate, warm and rather pleasant to the touch in the hot late-September sun, I could look up and see a convex bulge, like the side of a giant whale. It swelled up seventy feet to where straggling heather poked up like a crazed wig. The surface was a little cracked and seamed. There were sections that were rougher, broken, like the side of a huge, freshly cut, black parmesan, but it would have taken no more than a couple of hours with a grinder to smooth off every imperfection and leave a perfect finish.

'The whole approach has to be fluid,' Johnny explained. 'It's not so much a question of standing on things as moving across the face of it and using one hold to sort of propel yourself on to the next.'

'But I can't even see a starting point.'

Johnny peered at the slate and brushed the surface with his fingers. For a moment it looked as if he couldn't either. 'It's difficult to explain, but come here.' He led me sideways about twenty feet. 'This is a grade seven, which I did some years before the nine and, here, look, you could do this. You see, there, you put your foot in there…' – he fingered a rough slight hollow – '…but with a press and lift. It's a whole movement. You have to have a sideways thrust to allow you the momentum to get up.'

He lifted his foot and placed it against a slight bulge in the rock. 'You've got a good hold here,' he said, and reached up to place his fingers on a nubble above his head. 'But you have to use the friction to swing up and flat against the rock.' With a slight spring he swung upwards off the ground, launched his foot to the left, his fingers above his head, and slapped on to the rock like a gecko. 'You see,' he said, looking down at me over his shoulder, 'I didn't put my weight on the right foot at all really. I used it as a pivot.'

For the next fifteen minutes I tried over and over again to get on to this first position. I was wearing the same shoes, starting from the same point, pushing with the same swing, into the face of the rock. Johnny was a little shorter than me, but he didn't look spectacularly wiry or impossibly muscled. He could just stick to the stuff in a way that was impossible for me to replicate. My right foot slid off immediately, or my left foot crumpled or my fingers found nothing to grip. And, humiliatingly, this was at the very base. I could always step straight back down to the ground. I *had* to always step straight back to the ground. Unbelievably, Johnny Dawes not only got on to that limpet, splayed, friction-based hold, he could use it as a platform for another swing, via more minimally existent nodules, straight on and up the slithery face.

And he did just this, back at the severe climb, the number nine, the one without the easy start. It was fluid, liquid and apparently without effort and undertaken in sequences that hardly allowed time to think, let alone enjoy second thoughts.

I stood at the bottom nursing a temporary inability to close my mouth, while he arched, swung and pushed until he was about two-thirds up. 'So how much of this is prepared…?'

RIGHT: Jagged majesty. Inside the abandoned slate quarry.

'Just a minute, Griff,' he came back. 'I can't quite talk just at the moment.' This was the only sign that there was any complexity at all in what he was doing.

'No. I'll rest here. I hate this next bit.' He was now just under the top and leaning out a little from the wall on a couple of footholds that were impossible to see. 'Of course, we read and study the face,' he went on, 'but I genuinely believe that what I do brings me as close to the mountain as a human being can be. By climbing it I understand it.' He took some sharp breaths, grunted slightly and launched himself at the final overhanging slab. There was no scrabbling or heaving. The progression was simply balletic, like a rock dance. In a few more seconds he crossed the lip and a few seconds later his face poked back over the edge and looked down at me. 'Phew. I'm not sure I can do that more than a couple of times a day,' he said.

I found myself disputing 'the stone monkey's' nickname. I doubt that a monkey could have done what he did.

I was feeling more Welsh, daily. Betws-y-Coed, where we were staying, was, I discovered, pronounced 'Betoos-ee-Coyd'. It was just a few miles across the pass. Here there were salmon jumping in the stream by the bridge. The dry summer and the warm autumn had squirted a sudden yellow and red glow into the leaves. We were back in the wild places for tea.

It was interesting to head south the following day. We were going to meet Lawrence and Lez, who were running a new business under the shadow of Cadair Idris. Down towards Dolgellau the bare upper mountains gave way to wooded slopes. Suddenly the country closed in. There was raw, romantic excitement in the way the peaks struck up through the forest. 'Why not explore beyond our screen into the hidden places?' they seemed to be saying to me. Ah, that old selfish explorer gene. I love woods.

Rain hung in curtains of fizzy mist around the slopes. The sun broke through and rainbows arced past and dipped into the field next to the road.

Lez and Lawrence occupied a hut in another deserted slate quarry. Up to the west a huge cascade of grey shards fanned out down the side, topped by yellowing larches, and opposite the same waste heaps were flung out from huge cave mouths. I wanted to explore before we talked.

'Are we all right to walk up here?' I asked Lawrence.

'It's a criminal offence to climb on the mines, and you could fall over the edge and die,' he said. 'But I've been up there lots of times.' He laughed from the door of his hut.

I could hardly drag myself away from this quarry. When I first looked on mountains I remember being impressed by their amplitude. You couldn't make one with a JCB, I decided. But slate mining had changed my mind about this. Clearly, if you were a determined bunch of excavators then you could take a significant bite out of the side of any mountain. Snowdonia was riddled with the results. And most of it was waste. Ninety per cent of the process consisted of throwing stuff away. And they didn't throw it far.

At Aberllefenni they seemed to have dumped the left-overs right up to the edge of farmland. Loose grey shard spilled over towards a pretty spinney. Three horses

LEFT: Half a mountain munched away and scattered around a valley.

ran down and galloped in the field. The remains of towers and sheds stuck up, like strange monoliths, in the chaos; as if someone had decided to play about with all these spare black building blocks.

I walked up gingerly, following a track, and looked down on the remains of a winding tower, built haphazardly and abandoned as if on a whim. The original cables lay in a thread of bright rusting oxide through the grey. And even here there were tussocks of grass. How did it get a grip? The shattered slews were punctuated with lumps of heather or the occasional tree. Given a little time, nature would reclaim even this assault.

But I had other business here. Lawrence and Lez were engaged in a spot of recycling themselves. They had a single neatly proportioned shed with an incongruous King's Road image of a cartoon sheep carved into a slate plaque hanging in the apex. Inside, a workbench ran down the centre of the room. There were two battered washing machines at the far end. Pipes led off to a tank. On the left, under the window, were two large pots and a propane gas cylinder. To the right was another tank and wooden frames, like silk screens. Above the door, on carefully made hangers constructed out of stripped branches, flat flaps of rough paper hung to dry. This was what they made here. Paper made of sheep poo.

Lawrence was the entrepreneur. He and Lez wore chequered aprons. His quiff flopping down in front of his eyes, Lawrence put on a dazzling performance, taking me through each stage of the process: the sterilization, the triple wash to remove bacteria (providing recyclable liquid fertilizer), the tray of dried and washed sheep droppings – 'now smelling like fresh hay' – and his precious baby, the Holland machine, 'which runs a sludge of porridge through dual cutters to separate and shred the cellulose into long threads – rather than mash it like a liquidizer, you understand.'

He slid a tray, just a frame with a cloth bottom, into the tank of water, added a plastic measuring jug of the sheep-shit porridge, 'scotched' it with his fingertips so that it mixed thoroughly and then lifted the frame straight up and let it hang dripping. The water oozed out through the cloth bottom. Predictably, but nonetheless like magic, the porridge was now evenly spread in a thin smear all over the fabric at the bottom of the frame. It was this thin smear which, when allowed to dry, would be prised off, pressed flatter and become a sheet of paper.

Lez could make about 100 sheets a day by this method. There was a judge in Texas who had ordered a special paper enhanced with the hairs of her dog. But the main ingredient was sheep croppings.

Getting hold of this stuff was simple enough. Lez and I took a bucket and walked up to the blindingly green field a little way up the hill. First we had to dress in paper overalls. This was at the request of the farmer. Apparently like this we wouldn't scare the sheep. Though scaring the sheep might have produced what we were looking for a little more quickly, I would have thought.

As well as being able to tell my children what flowers we pass, what rocks we see and what birds we observe on a walk, I am now in the position to tell them which sheep shit is fresh, to point out how the beetles have invaded some, how others have exploded unto useless pulp, but the good stuff is spread like chocolate buttons. 'It only takes an afternoon,' Lez told me. He pointed into his bucket. 'I've got enough for fifteen or so pages already.'

Back at the hut I made my own piece of paper. Odourless and a pallid grey, it

ABOVE: The farmer ordered us to pick up droppings disguised as sheep.

was hung up to dry and Lawrence said he would send it on to me later. They sell a lot of greetings cards. I imagine they might have problems with repeat business. Perhaps they should make special pads for writing letters of complaint. 'Dear sir, this letter is written on shit, but compared with the service I got on your train to Liverpool on Sunday night…'

Tryfan is moderately commanding. By no means the highest mountain in Wales, it has an excellent primitive physique: slopey at the bottom and rising to a sharp, pointy point.

We were back north for this, my final ascent. I was still confused by the roads at valley level. I had worked out that the one that heads round the lake and then dips into a valley full of interesting boulders was the Llanberis Pass, but somewhere along the way we took a right and now entered another valley, similarly sheep-shorn, but less cluttered. George Band was in the car with me, dressed elegantly for climbing in a sort of cravat and knickerbockers over red socks.

Born in Taiwan in 1929, George had begun climbing as a student and in 1955

was the first to climb Kangchenjunga, the world's third-highest peak, leaving the top ten feet undisturbed out of respect for the Sikkimese, who considered the mountain sacred. But two years before, when he was twenty-four, George had been the youngest member of Sir John Hunt's 1953 Everest expedition. Now he was going to lead me up Tryfan. As we drove up to the car park he pointed to two climbers at the top of the craggy ridge. 'Adam and Eve,' he explained. They weren't climbers. I was not the first to make the boob. They were pillar rocks on the very summit of the mountain. They are very much bigger than human beings in reality, but from the bottom they looked like two watchers on the peak.

'I'm not sure which is which,' George continued. 'You're supposed to leap from one to the other to indicate your supremacy of Tryfan.'

George had less natty climbing stuff with him. It was well worn and slightly faded but it also sported the legend 'Adidas' in big letters, so the BBC fussed about it a bit. We found another jacket and we began to trudge.

It was not hard going. We slipped past a perfect wall of granite. This was not George's usual route so he was interested to be led on. 'I walked with the family a while back,' he said. 'We took the Heather Terrace path.' He pointed upwards. 'You see the ridge. It goes along underneath and on round the side.'

I nodded, I was still not really sure if I had read the mountain correctly, but I deferred to George. Who wouldn't? As we skirted past some of the feral goats sporting horns of regimental mascot proportions that live up here, George explained that before the Everest ascent they had come to Tryfan, 'not to train exactly, because we had to be pretty experienced mountaineers to be chosen, but to practise with the oxygen gear, which was new to us.'

George had become the president of the Cambridge University Climbing Club and already led teams into the Alps. When they advertised for Everest expedition members he decided to throw his bobble hat into the ring.

We stopped and rested on a ridge where an enormous slab of rock jutted out over the valley. For the sake of a picture I clambered out along it. It was called 'the cannon'. 'Because you need balls to do it,' I suggested. Though you didn't. It wasn't very frightening, but it looked it, which was the point.

George had brought some of his original kit, including string long johns. It dated me and him. I had worn string vests to school, when they came with the

LEFT: It's called 'the cannon' because you need balls to climb it.

imprimatur of the commandos, and all twelve-year-olds had to have them. His jacket was a magnificently faded bit of nylon, spattered with paint. I upbraided him, 'How can you have used these for painting? They should be in a museum!'

'Well, they were. They've been in and out of museums, but I had some odd jobs to attend to.'

George was a wonderfully sane companion, loving the climb, loving the view on this clear afternoon, pointing out the hostel where they had set up a camp, below in a little fuzz of trees, and climbing with a steady pace up the lower paths. 'In fact we were very well supplied with all the latest stuff. There was quite a lot riding on it.'

Back in the early fifties the French and the Swiss were preparing teams too. Everest has been described as 'the third pole'. Britain felt it had failed in the Antarctic partly because of bad equipment. Now, with the coronation of the Queen about to happen, there must have been a little extra edge to the proceedings.

'Yes, but a lot of that came later. The newspapers built that up. We didn't feel enormously patriotic or anything. In fact, when we got to the British Ambassador's residence, at some party before we left, he asked us if we had a flag … and we didn't.' George was the sort of chap who really did throw back his head to laugh. 'So he gave us the Union Jack off his Rolls-Royce. That was the actual flag that Tenzing is holding in the famous picture.'

We clambered on. Soon the grass stopped and Tryfan became a scramble, which is to say the mountain turned into a magnificent jumble of heaped rocks, one on top of the other, piling ever upwards, hundreds and hundreds of feet on. Perhaps it is because it is so pointed, or perhaps because of the particular form of taupe granite that it is made of, but Tryfan became the most exciting climbing frame that I had ever attacked. Up to then we had taken our time. George had preferred not to try to talk while on the steeper bits and I deferred to his age, but now that he could use his hands, and his commanding height, he began to forge away.

'George,' I moaned. 'You'll have to slow a bit. I'm fifty-two.'

But I could feel it too. It was a wonderful scramble, nothing physically daunting, and no hanging, dangling or teetering; just a firm sense of progression,

RIGHT: George points out the Everest team headquarters in the valley below Tryfan.

up and over a continuous pile of giant shards, satisfying and involving and leading, after another hour, to a high stone field. Ahead of us, totally improbably, stood the two pillars of Adam and Eve. Each projected about ten feet into the air from the very pinnacle, as if there were twin cords of rock running right through the mountain, like iron bars through a block of reinforced concrete. A high, cold wind was now blowing, but it cleared the air and the distance. Unlike Snowdon, there was no one else around. The nearest other human beings were in those tiny silver-mercury blobs of cars slipping along the black thread of the road thousands of feet below.

I grappled with the top of Adam, or possibly Eve, and heaved myself inelegantly up the smooth sides on to what seemed a horribly unsafe top. I wasn't going to stand but George did, momentarily, on the other one. 'That was a good climb, an excellent climb,' he said. 'I've never come that route before. It was very enjoyable.' And for a moment we sat and stared out, our reward for our effort.

George had climbed many mountains. He had been with the first expedition to the highest mountain in the world. He had made the first ascents of famous peaks

ABOVE: Respect for the mountain should be interpreted as respect for each other.

in remote places. But sitting on that rock he was happy to acknowledge that this was as good as it gets. The view was great, the climb had been thrilling, and, even if we were threatening to slip to our doom because of the number who had polished our seats to glass, there were none of them there at that moment. For a minute or two we were in a wild place, like the first in time.

There are millions who want something from these uplands – day trips, homes, scientific knowledge, jobs, challenges, thrills, holidays, photographs, energy (spiritual and electrical), memories, souvenir shops and even utter solitude. Over the past months I had discovered that the list is various and endless. There is a lot more to mountains than climbing them.

At that moment, as we sat there, the mountain ranges stretching away, illuminated with gold, the upper world looked almost big enough to absorb each of these desires, but I knew that it needed 'respect'. People talk airily of 'respecting the mountain', but the mountain will look after itself long after we are gone. It will rise again, if not here, then on some other planet, in some other galaxy, on some other molten crust, in a billion, billion years. Nature has its own inexorable timetable. We don't. 'Respect for the mountain' in the context of our minuscule time in space really means respect for other human beings. Surely people can only have whatever they want here as long as they understand what others want too and do nothing which will grossly interfere with that. Every age imagines emergencies and crises. Every age has its priorities. They might be slate roofs or power stations or renewable energy, cafés, power lines, houses or climbing walls. The 'urgent need' changes every ten years. But if we allow each generation to make its 'necessary', 'urgent', 'crisis-driven' incursions then we will steadily erode what we can get from these extraordinary places, as surely as the ice and snow erode the stone. Except that we will make it happen a lot more quickly.

It was time to go down. To take the jarring, juddering path again.

And when the bottom comes, when the car park comes, you bless asphalt. You rival the Pope in your desire to bend and kiss tarmac – a soft, relenting, smooth surface at last. You feel like a hovercraft – drifting and sliding over the blessed blacktop.

After two, perhaps three hours, here is the horizontal world.

INDEX

Note: page numbers in italics refer to illustrations

PICTURE CREDITS

ACKNOWLEDGEMENTS

Without sounding like an Oscar speech, there are too many people to thank for the work that went into making this book. The teams who put together the individual television programmes were exemplary. The brilliant directors, diligent assistant producers and hard-working researchers who made it happen did a splendid job. With sound and cameramen who walked or climbed a lot further than I did; with a team of dedicated safety people who carried tons of gear and, quite frequently, me; with back-up from the office, drivers, helicopter pilots and editors – it sounds like a veritable army of support for one man's hill-walk, and it was, but I thank you all. I may have rendered you largely invisible in here but I valued everything you did. Hamish, Franny, Andrea and Ian have led from the front and Paul, Kate and Miriam have stepped forward to help with the book in many selfless ways, so I do want to thank you particularly. Rowland, Richard and Carly at Michael Joseph, and Fiona at Essential Works, have been dogged and charming on the publishing front. Cat has listened graciously as ever, and my wife Jo has done all the slog and missed all the summits. I dedicate this book to all of you. I made some real friends climbing mountains. Thank you.